HELP!
For Elementary School Substitutes and Beginning Teachers

Help!
For
Elementary School
Substitutes
and
Beginning Teachers

Text and Illustrations by
MARY LOU MORROW

THE WESTMINSTER PRESS
Philadelphia

COPYRIGHT © 1974 THE WESTMINSTER PRESS

<u>All rights reserved</u> - no part of this book may be reproduced in any form without permission in writing from the publisher, except by a reviewer who wishes to quote brief passages in connection with a review in magazine or newspaper.

Published by The Westminster Press®
Philadelphia, Pennsylvania

PRINTED IN THE UNITED STATES OF AMERICA

<u>Library of Congress Cataloging in Publication Data</u>

Morrow, Mary Lou, 1926-
   Help! For elementary school substitutes and beginning teachers.

   1. Language arts (Elementary) - Handbooks, manuals, etc. 2. Educational games - Handbooks, manuals, etc. 3. Arts - Study and teaching (Elementary) - Handbooks, manuals, etc. 4. Mathematics - Study and teaching (Elementary) - Handbooks, manuals, etc. I. Title.
LB1576.M8   372.1'3   73-22029
ISBN 0-664-24984-1

To my father,
Stanford Hannah,
    a dedicated educator;
and to my mother,
Bernice Hannah,
    a dedicated wife and mother

Contents

INTRODUCTION — 9
    To the beginning elementary school substitute teacher — 9
    To the experienced elementary school substitute teacher — 10
    On discipline — 11
    How to begin the day — 13

IDEAS AND ACTIVITIES FOR KINDERGARTEN THROUGH SECOND GRADE — 17
    Reading and phonics activities — 17
        Individual phonics seatwork — 17
        Class phonics drills and games — 22
    Language arts activities — 27
        Individual seatwork — 27
        Class activities and drills — 30
    Math games and drills — 31

IDEAS AND ACTIVITIES FOR THIRD THROUGH FIFTH GRADES — 33
    Reading activities — 33
        Individual seatwork — 33
        Class reading activities — 34
    Language arts activities — 37
        Individual seatwork — 37
        Class games and drills — 39
    Math games and drills — 43

RELAXER MOVEMENTS, PANTOMIMES,
  AND DISCUSSION OPENERS   47
    Relaxer movements   47
    Pantomimes   50
    Discussion openers   56

GAMES   61
    Indoor games   61
    Outdoor games   68

ARTS AND CRAFTS   73
    Simple ideas for younger children, graduating
      to more complex for older children   73
    Seasonal arts and crafts, including holidays   92
        Autumn   92
           Fall holiday ideas   95
        Winter   105
           Winter holiday ideas   107
           Christmas   107
           Valentine's Day   115
        Spring   116

OUTLINES FOR PATTERNS OR DUPLICATING MASTERS   123

Introduction

TO THE BEGINNING ELEMENTARY SCHOOL SUBSTITUTE TEACHER

Welcome to a challenging, stimulating, and rewarding experience. It takes a special kind of person to enjoy and succeed at being a substitute teacher - one who sincerely likes children, and is patient, creative, and versatile.

This book has been designed to be a handy collection of ideas and activities for reading, phonics, language arts, games (indoor and outdoor), math, and, especially, arts and crafts. These all are ideas that have been collected over many years of substituting and teaching and have proved to be the most workable, the easiest to present, and of the most interest to the pupils. The time-consuming job of searching through educational books and magazines for useful, practical activities, ones that require little or no special preparation and materials, has been done for you. You have the assurance that only the ideas which were used with success over and over are included here.

This teaching aid is convenient and compact. When you receive an early morning phone call requesting you to substitute, it would be much more convenient to pick up this book than a collection of the magazine with the Halloween craft idea, the envelope with the witch patterns, the poetry book that has the ghost poem, the booklet on math drills, the pamphlet on outdoor games, and the paperback book on language arts activities for elementary school pupils.

Confidence is of great importance to a substitute, since the pupils, even the youngest ones, know when the substitute is insecure, and they behave accordingly. This book will help boost your confidence by giving you the assurance that at your fingertips are many activities that you know can be used readily and successfully.

Many of the suggested ideas and activities can be used to reinforce the children's regular lessons. Others are creative or "just for fun" ideas. The latter are often best used at the end of the day, when all the assigned lessons are completed. It is remarkable to see how quietly and eagerly the class can finish its regular assignments when looking forward to the treat of "something different."

As a substitute teacher, with your own ideas and methods, you can provide a refreshing change in the class's routine schedule. There is a great feeling of satisfaction when, upon arriving at the assigned classroom, you - a confident, cheerful, resourceful substitute - overhear: "Oh, good! We get Mrs. Smith today!"

TO THE EXPERIENCED ELEMENTARY SCHOOL SUBSTITUTE TEACHER

Since you have already done substitute teaching, you know how you feel when the telephone rings during breakfast. (Why is it the bell sounds so much louder and more shrill then?) The harsh ring makes your pulse leap and your nerves jangle. On the way to the phone you mumble, "Where to today?" And you wonder what grade level - kindergarten that demands so much of you, physically, or a battle-of-the-wits fifth grade? You soon learn that Mrs. Treadwell (third grade, Parkhill School) has a virus and will be out at least two days. As you hastily begin removing hair rollers, you wonder, "Is that the class 'Clarence the Clown' is in? Let's see, now, Mrs. Treadwell's specialty is music. (Your weak point, of course.) What can I do to fill up the time scheduled for choral practice? Maybe we could do something for Columbus Day. It's coming up soon."

So while directing your own children to clear off their breakfast dishes and get ready for school, you begin dressing, thinking: "I'll take that ditto master of Columbus' ships. Now where did I put that green book of poems? There is a poem in it on Columbus, I think. Let's see, third grade, I'll have to find my book of language arts for that level. And last month's teacher's magazine had a couple of interesting-sounding ideas in it I wanted to try out." By the time you have gathered up what you need, it's a rather cumbersome load to carry, and you will still need to search through it for the appropriate pages and projects after you are in the classroom.

As an elementary school substitute and teacher of many years, I realize the need for a single, compact, easy-to-use book of activities for classroom use, ones that need little or no preparation and can be quickly and easily found. All the ideas in this book have been used over and over and are interesting and easy to present. As an addition to your own collection of useful materials, may it aid in giving you the confidence of knowing that you are well prepared to meet the challenges of the day.

ON DISCIPLINE

It has been taught that a beginning teacher or a substitute should be quite strict at first, since it is easier to relax discipline later than it is to tighten up discipline after originally establishing an easygoing atmosphere. There is merit in the policy that a new teacher should let it firmly be known, from the start, just what type of behavior and classwork is expected. However, this should be accomplished in a friendly manner so as not to alienate the children.

As with parent-child relationships, the preferred atmosphere is one in which the children behave and respond in a positive way because they like and respect the adults involved, rather than because they fear the consequences if they misbehave or fail to do what is expected of them. The teacher can be firm, yet be fair, friendly, soft-spoken, a willing listener, and can impart a feeling to the children of "being on their side."

Whenever possible, praise the class for its industriousness, compliment a group on its quietness, or thank a pupil for his cooperation. When the children are working quietly let them know that you are leaving a note for their teacher which will include compliments on their behavior. Do this early in the day, as a few words of praise can do wonders.

Occasionally, in spite of your best efforts, there are troublemakers determined to upset the substitute. In private, firmly inform the disrupting child that you dislike this sort of behavior and will not allow it to interrupt the class. Assure him that it is the behavior you dislike rather than the child. Tell him that he will be asked to leave the room unless he settles down. If he continues to disrupt the class, insist that he leave the room, either to go to the office or to take a book and sit on a chair just outside the door. Carrying out this discipline in a calm, yet firm manner should discourage other potential behavior problems. Let it be known that, unfortunately, such episodes will have to be described in your note to their teacher.

Since young children respond to the positive traits of the substitute, strive to:

- have a sense of humor
- be fair
- recognize and praise the children's good behavior
- compliment the class on its effort
- give encouragement
- develop efficiency in presenting class lessons
- show personal interest in individuals
- be an understanding listener
- be pleasant and friendly
- use a relaxed, quiet speaking voice.

HOW TO BEGIN THE DAY

The following step-by-step example of "setting the stage" for a successful day was used by the author in a variety of schools in several different communities, and most often proved to be quite workable.

Arrive at the school as early as possible, sign in, and obtain the location of the classroom and its key. Check the absent teacher's box for materials or notices that might be pertinent to your day. Glance over the office bulletin board and check on any special duties, such as yard or bus duties.

On arriving in the classroom, first look for a lesson plan book on or in the teacher's desk, and quickly scan through the plans for the day. Then study more carefully the plans for the first period. Look for fire drill instructions in the plan book or posted on a wall. Next, take a quick tour of the room, locating materials such as flash cards, paper, art supplies, and teacher editions of textbooks. Open windows as needed.

By now a few children may have arrived. Choose two to stay in the room to help you. Then, weather and yard supervision permitting, lock the door, ignoring the knocks and calls of the children. Learn the first names of your two helpers and let them know how much you appreciate their helping you. This will put two members of the class on your side before class even begins. Ask your helpers any questions you might have on the procedure of the first period and on how the opening routine is handled - flag salute, roll, lunch and milk counts, absentee excuses, and whether monitors do any of these tasks. Try to determine as closely as possible the exact opening routine, because the class will respect a substitute who conducts the opening in the manner with which they are familiar. The children will have more confidence in a substitute who has made the effort to learn their routine than in one who conducts the opening in an entirely unfamiliar way.

Also, before class begins, have the two helpers bring you five or six sheets of light-colored or manila construction paper. Cut these in half lengthwise, then in thirds horizontally, so that each sheet is cut into six pieces. Have the helpers place one piece on each desk, to be used for name tags. Now write assignments as found in the plan book on the blackboard, and include an extra assignment of your own choosing for those who may finish the regular work early. In one upper corner of the board, write your own name.

When it is time to open the door for the class, stand by the door, or outside the door if the class lines up outside before entering, and smile. Allow the children to come in quietly. Keep any who are not settled down from coming in until they are quiet and ready. When most of the pupils are in, go to the front of the class and wait a few seconds until all the children are seated and quiet. Welcome them cheerfully and tell them that since their teacher is absent, you will be working with them today. If possible, tell them why their teacher is absent. Give your name, and point to it on the board. Explain to them that in order to help them and their teacher, you would like to cover as much of the lessons planned as possible, but that probably several things will be done differently or will be omitted, since you are not the same person as their teacher. Tell the class that you would welcome any suggestions or information on how they usually go about various aspects of their day.

Have the children fold lengthwise the pieces of paper they find on their desks and boldly print their first names on them with a dark crayon. If there are two or more children with the same first name, have these add a last initial. Instruct them to stand the cards on the front of their desk tops, with the names facing the front of the room. Ask one child to go around the room tearing off and passing out pieces of cellophane tape to be used for securing the name tags to the desks. Proceed with the opening business. Announce that if there is time left at the end of the day after all the assignments are completed, you will try to give the class something different and fun to do, such as games or arts and crafts. This often serves as an incentive to them to keep busy and not waste time, especially if they are reminded, during times when they are working well, that it looks as though there will be time to do something that is fun.

Try not to have any periods of time during which the children have nothing to do. Get assignments going as soon as possible. It helps to have the assignments written on the board in the order in which they are to be done, concluding with a few extra choices for those who finish early. Use recesses and part of the lunch period to prepare further for the next lessons, and step by step you <u>will</u> make it!

Ideas and Activities for Kindergarten Through Second Grade

READING AND PHONICS ACTIVITIES

INDIVIDUAL PHONICS SEATWORK

Phonics Draw

Have the pupils fold a piece of paper into fourths and then open it up again. Instruct the class to write one consonant at the bottom of each block formed by the fold lines. These consonants could be of the children's own choosing, or you could put them on the blackboard, to be copied in each block. Then in each block have the children draw something that begins with this consonant. The four blocks on the reverse side may also be used.

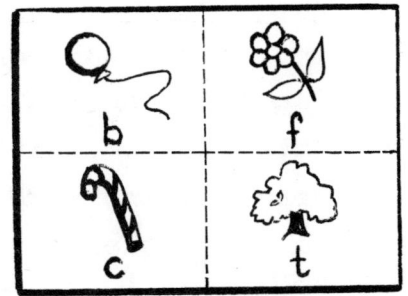

Phonics Picture

Instruct the children to draw and color an original picture containing several things that begin with a given consonant. For instance, if the consonant is l, the picture might contain a ladybug on a leaf by a lady holding a letter, and a lad holding a lollipop and a toy lion. The pupils could choose someone to find as many of these objects as he can in their picture.

"b"

Rhyming Match

Write a list of simple words on the board. Next to the list, make a second column of rhyming words, but in different sequence. Have the children copy the lists on their own paper and then find and match rhyming words by connecting them with lines. Do one or two with the class for an example.

```
say      pan
pin      sing
hot      take
saw      day
ring     not
hand     fin
ran      sand
make     paw
```

Choose the Right Rhyme

Have the class copy sentences, such as the following, from the blackboard, using only one of the rhyming words in the parentheses, so that the sentences make good sense. "Clue" pictures drawn at the end of each sentence may be used.

Example:
1. A duck has big (beet, feet).
2. A bird can (fly, sly).
3. The (dish, fish) can swim.
4. A clown has a funny (face, race).
5. The (tire, fire) is hot.

Phonics List Match

Draw five pictures on the blackboard with a numeral under each one. Then write three columns of one-syllable words, each with a short line at the end, as shown. Have the children copy the word lists and add the numeral that is under the picture which contains the same vowel sound. This may be used as a dittoed work sheet.

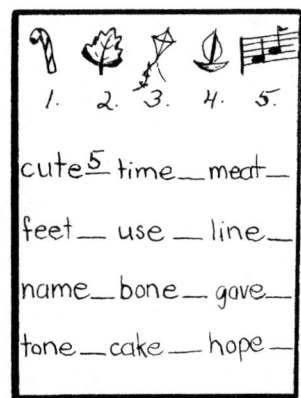

Missing Consonants

Write several simple sentences on the blackboard, leaving out a few initial consonants. Draw "clue" pictures at the end of each sentence as a help to the children in guessing the missing letters. Have the children copy these sentences and put in the missing consonants. This might be done as a dittoed work sheet.

Example:

1. Tom has a __agon and a __all.

2. I see a __ig and a __orse.

3. When the __un is down, I go to __ed.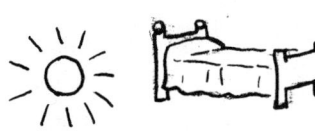

Vowel Sound Pictures

Have the pupils fold paper into thirds each way, then open it, forming nine blocks. Then have them copy nine simple pictures, which you have put on the board, one in each block. Under each picture have them write the vowel that they hear when pronouncing the name of that object, marking the vowel long or short.

Initial Consonants

Have the class copy simple word endings from the board and then write in an initial consonant that will complete a word. Have several pupils read their lists aloud.

Picture Rhyming

Ditto, or draw on the blackboard, simple pictures of objects that have rhyming names, two pictures in each block. Write the name under one of the pictures of each pair, and leave a space under the other. Have the children fold a piece of paper into fourths and copy the pictures and words, writing the rhyming words in the spaces.

20

Following Directions

Give each pupil an unlined piece of paper and tell him to follow carefully the written directions on the board. Make the direction sentences suitable to the grade level. The following example might be used in the first grade.

1. Make a big
2. Make five green on the tree
3. Draw a red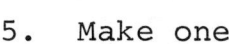
4. Color six blue
5. Make one
6. Draw three orange
7. Color two yellow

Finding Words

Designate the type of words to be searched for, such as ones that begin with a given consonant, contain a certain vowel sound, have an <u>ed</u> or <u>ing</u> ending. Write on the board the title of the story (or give the pages) in their reading books in which they will look for the words. The pupil with the longest list after a set time reads his list aloud.

CLASS PHONICS DRILLS AND GAMES

Climb the Ladder

Draw a large ladder on the blackboard. On each rung, write a vowel (or a consonant, or a blend). Choose a child to pronounce each sound, beginning from the bottom rung and "climbing the ladder." If he succeeds in reaching the top, he may be the pointer for the next child trying the climb.

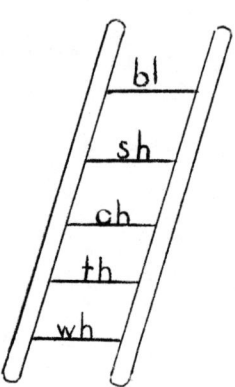

Phonics Slide

Draw a large slide with a stick figure at the top and place along the contour of the slide a series of sounds being studied. The children help the figure at the top to slide down by correctly pronouncing the sounds from top to bottom. If a child succeeds, with no mistakes, he becomes the next pointer. This same idea can be used with a hill to climb to reach the castle, or stair-steps reaching a treasure room, etc.

Phonics Picture

Draw on the blackboard a simple picture containing several items. Have the pupils come to the board one at a time and pronounce the name of an object. They then write that initial consonant on the object.

Phonics Wheel Drill

Draw a large circle on the blackboard. Mark off several sections, spoke-fashion. Write one consonant in each section, near the center. Choose one pupil at a time to come to the board. He must select one of the consonants, pronounce its sound, then sketch, in the same section, an object beginning with this sound.

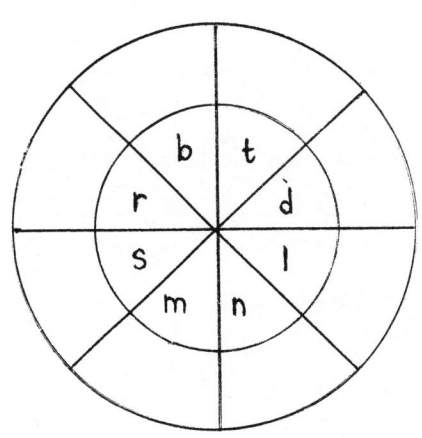

Phonics Memory

Draw on the blackboard several items that have names which begin with a letter sound that is currently being studied. After allowing the class to study the pictures for several seconds, erase them. See how many of the objects the children can list, orally or on paper.

Story Puzzle

Have the class dictate a paragraph of timely interest, which you write on the blackboard. Ask several pupils to read it aloud, so the class will become familiar with it. Now erase a few initial consonants or important vowels. Have several more pupils read the paragraph aloud and pronounce the sounds of the missing letters. The class should now be eager to attempt to copy the paragraph on paper, as a puzzle, trying to remember and write in all the missing letters.

Feeling Phonics

Have one child trace the outline of a letter on a second child's back. The second child must name the letter, give its sound, and pronounce a word that begins with the sound. If he is correct, he may be the next guesser.

Flash Card Placement

Put several consonant flash cards in the chalk tray in front of the class. Call on a pupil to come forward, take one letter card and place it against or beside an object in the room beginning with that sound. The pupil repeats this, until each letter card has been placed. If someone notices a mistake, he may raise his hand, and if he can point out and correct the mistake, he will get the next turn.

Phonics Guessing Game

Have a child come to the front of the classroom, whisper to the teacher a word of a predetermined category, such as a toy he wants for Christmas, a food, something we see in the spring, a classmate's first name. The child then writes the initial consonant on the board and calls on his classmates to guess his secret word. The one who guesses it writes the next letter on the board. Stress that the one up front should call only on the ones who are sitting quietly, with their hands raised.

Consonant Bingo

Instruct each pupil to fold his sheet of paper into fourths each way, then to open it. The folds will outline sixteen squares. Call out sixteen consonants, having the children write each one in any square, at random. (No two papers should have the letters in the same squares.) See that each child has several markers. These can be bits of paper, beans, etc. Then pronounce a word that begins with one of the given consonants, and each pupil covers this letter on his paper. When someone has four in a row covered, he calls, "Bingo!" He should then uncover the consonants that form the row, naming each and pronouncing its sound. You should have a prepared list of words in order to check each word as it is dictated, so that you can check the letters that form the winner's row.

Vowel Race

Write the five vowels in large letters on the blackboard. Choose two pupils, give them each a ruler for a pointer, and have them stand on opposite sides of the vowels. Pronounce a word containing one short vowel sound. The two children race to point first to the vowel whose sound was heard in the word. The loser chooses someone to take his place. If a child has three wins in a row, he should choose another pupil to take his place. Once a vowel is pointed to, there can be no changing to another choice.

Conductor

Choose one child to be conductor and have him stand beside the first pupil in the first row. Using vowel or consonant (or both) flash cards, hold up a card. The conductor and the child he is standing beside race to pronounce the sound of the letter on the flash card. The winner must give a word that begins with this sound. If the conductor wins, he moves to a position next to the second pupil in the row and challenges him. If the conductor loses, he is seated and the one who beat him becomes the new conductor. In case of a tie, flash another card.

Muffin Man Consonant Drill

Place consonant flash cards in the chalk tray in front of the class or write the consonants on the board. Choose one pupil to come to the front of the class and instruct him to listen closely while you sing, "Oh, do you know the muffin man . . .?" etc. The child then picks up or points to the letter m, for muffin. Now sing, to the same tune, "Oh, do you know the laundryman . . .?" He should then designate the l for laundry. Repeat, substituting such words as popcorn man, boogeyman, dancing man, happy man, jolly man, raggedy man. If the child chooses a wrong consonant, select another child to be It.

LANGUAGE ARTS ACTIVITIES

INDIVIDUAL SEATWORK

Adjective Drawing

Use this activity in teaching about descriptive words. Have the children fold a sheet of unlined paper into fourths, then open it. In each of the four blocks, have them draw something that can be described by an adjective you have named. Examples: cold, noisy, big, scary, funny, red, edible, etc.

"cold"

Poetry

Write a short poem on the board. This could be a favorite of yours, or one found in a literature book in the classroom, or one of the children's favorite rhymes dictated to you. Read the poem several times with the class and discuss it, if desired. Have the pupils carefully copy the poem and illustrate it.

Spelling Word Directions

Have the children fold a piece of paper into fourths to form four squares. Write four sentences on the board, using as many current spelling words as possible. The pupils draw one picture in each square, illustrating these sentences.

Fantastic Animals

Encourage the children to draw a very imaginary animal. Instruct them to be prepared to describe their animal to the class by telling where the animal can be found, what it eats, its name, its habits, why no one has ever seen one before, etc. This description could be a written one.

Correct the Teacher

Write several sentences on the board, using no punctuation or capitals. Have the class copy the sentences, putting in the correct punctuation marks and capital letters. The sentences might be chosen from a spelling lesson, the reading books, or a social studies lesson.

Complete the Sentences

Write sentence beginnings on the board. Have the pupils copy these and complete the sentences in their own words. Encourage the pupils to use as many words as they need to make an interesting sentence. Example:

1. Are you _____?

2. Where is _____?

3. That little bird _____.

4. One day I _____.

5. I like to _____.

6. Is that _____?

Alphabetical Order

Write spelling words, or any given list of words, on the board. These could be from the word list at the end of a reading book, color words, children's first names, etc. Have the pupils write the words in alphabetical order.

CLASS ACTIVITIES AND DRILLS

Drama

Divide the class into groups of three or four. Give each group several objects (ball, eraser, cap, scarf, plant, calendar, etc.). Each group then plans and presents an original skit, using these objects as props in its story.

Spelling Password

List spelling words on the board. Choose a pointer and a guesser. The guesser stands with his back to the board. The pointer points to a word, and the pupils take note of which word it is. They raise their hands if they have in mind a one-word clue to help the guesser determine which word was pointed to. The guesser calls on a total of three classmates for clues (one from each), and is allowed three guesses. If he guesses the word, he must spell it aloud correctly. After three successful turns, the guesser chooses the next guesser and the pointer chooses a new pointer. New guesser and pointer are chosen after each failure to guess the word or to spell it correctly.

Dictation Race

Divide the class into two teams. One member from each team comes to the board and takes a piece of chalk. As you dictate a simple sentence, the two children write it on the board. Award one point to the team whose member had the fewer errors in his sentence.

Correct the Paragraph

Write a paragraph on the board with several words misspelled and with some of the punctuation incorrect or left out. Have the children raise their hands when they discover an error and, when you call on them, come to the board and correct that error. Each child may correct just one mistake. Have the class continue until the paragraph is correct.

MATH GAMES AND DRILLS

Ball Bounce

Have the children put their heads on their desk tops and close their eyes. At the back of the room, bounce a ball. Have the pupils raise their hands to tell how many bounces were heard. This is a good drill to quiet down the class. Ball bounces can be done in combinations, such as four bounces, a pause, then two more bounces. The child must say, "Four plus two equals six."

Make the Number

Use two sets of flash cards, each set showing the numerals zero through nine. Two teams of ten pupils line up, one team on each side of the room, each pupil holding a number card. The teacher calls out a number, such as seven hundred and fifty-six. The team members on each side who are holding a card showing one of the digits in the number called step to the middle front of the class and hold their cards up in the correct order to form the number. Award a point for the team that first forms the number correctly. Larger or smaller numbers of digits may be used.

Conductor

Choose one pupil to be the conductor and have him stand beside the first child in the first row, both facing you. Flash a card showing an addition or a subtraction problem. The pupil who responds first with the correct answer becomes the conductor and moves on to challenge the next pupil in the row. In case of a tie, present another number problem.

Number Memory

With the children holding their pencils high, read aloud a four-digit to six-digit number. At the signal, "Begin," each pupil writes the number on his paper. After ten or so have been written, have the class exchange papers and check.

Visual Math

Demonstrate the principles of addition and subtraction by using the children themselves, or objects in the room. For example, ask three girls to stand up in the front of the classroom and say, "We have three girls now." Then ask two boys to come up front and tell the class: "We are adding two more children to the group we already had. Now let's count and see how many children there are altogether in the group (or set)." Then ask: "What would happen if we took away, or subtracted, two people from our set of five? How many are left? What is a number sentence that would tell about what we just did?"
Many number sentences can be demonstrated in such a way, letting the children manipulate objects to form sets by addition and subtraction.

Ideas and Activities for Third Through Fifth Grades

<u>READING ACTIVITIES</u>

INDIVIDUAL SEATWORK

<u>Who Am I?</u>
Each pupil picks a character from a given story and writes several descriptive sentences about him. These are read aloud to the class later as a guessing game.

<u>Endings</u>
From pages designated by the teacher, the pupils list all the words that have endings. The roots, or base parts of the words, are to be underlined.

<u>Blends</u>
From designated pages, the pupils list all the words that begin or end with blends. These blends are to be underlined.

<u>Vowels</u>
From designated pages, the pupils make a list of words that contain long vowel sounds and put a mark over the long vowels. This can be done using short vowels.

<u>Syllables</u>
From a group of pages designated by the teacher, the pupils list as many two-syllable words as they can find, dividing the words into syllables and marking the accent.

<u>What Did He Do?</u>
The pupils make a list of all the characters in a story they have just read. Then they write a one-sentence description of what each person (or animal) did in the story.

What Is Happening?

Each pupil folds an unlined sheet of paper into fourths, then opens it. In each of the four sections, he draws a picture showing an event that happened in a story he has just read. The child writes one sentence under each picture, telling what is happening.

CLASS READING ACTIVITIES

Read Aloud

One pupil is chosen to begin reading a story aloud to the class. If he makes an error, another pupil may raise his hand and be called on by the teacher to make the correction. This person then becomes the new reader. If a reader comes to a word he doesn't know, the teacher may pronounce it for him and it is not a mistake. Nor is it a mistake when the reader stammers over a word, but gets it correct by figuring and sounding it out on his own. It is a mistake when the reader gives a wrong word or leaves one out, puts in a word that is not there, gives a wrong tense or ending on a word, etc.

Parts

If a story has a section with a lot of dialogue, it is interesting to assign parts to the children, stressing that they should leave out the "he said's," etc., between the quotations in the story. It is usually necessary to assign a "reader" to read the sentences that are not conversation.

Who Am I?

The children take turns coming to the front of the classroom and giving two or three sentences describing a character in a recently read story, then choosing someone to guess which character it is.

Answer Search

The children have their books open to the same page. The teacher asks a question about something on this page. The first child to find the sentence that answers the question is called on to read it aloud.

Phonics T Race

Two contestants come to the blackboard and each makes a large T shape on the board. Down the left side of the T, in a column, they write five or six consonants, pronounced by the teacher. The teacher then names a vowel and the contestants write it above their T and proceed to race by putting a consonant along the right side of the T that completes a word. The word is formed by the top letter of the column on the left of the T, plus the vowel above, plus the top letter of the right column. The contestants continue, using the second letters of the columns. The one who finishes first, with correct words, remains at the board, and the teacher chooses a new challenger.

Phonics Race

This drill requires two teams of players and a stopwatch. The teacher names a common consonant. The first child on Team A says as many words as he can think of that begin with this letter. He is given a time limit, such as thirty seconds by the stopwatch. The number of correct words is recorded on the blackboard under his team's name. The teacher then gives Team B a consonant. When every team member has had a turn, the teacher adds the score to determine the winning team.

Grocery Phonics

The teacher writes an appropriate phrase in large capital letters on the blackboard. The phrase might be "WELCOME BACK," "HAPPY BIRTHDAY,_____," "MERRY CHRISTMAS," etc. The children take turns coming to the board and saying, "I went to the store and bought some _____," naming something found in a grocery store. The item must start with one of the letters in the phrase. The child then erases this letter and is seated. The activity continues until all the letters have been erased.

Consonant Bingo

The children fold a piece of paper into fourths each way, then open it, forming sixteen squares. They then write teacher-dictated consonants in each square, at random, so that each paper will be different. Each pupil needs bits of torn paper or other markers. The teach pronounces a word and the pupils cover the beginning consonant on their papers with a marker. The first child to have four letters in a row covered with markers calls out, "Bingo!" Instead of consonants, blends or digraphs could be used.

Alphabet Game

The children sit on the floor or the ground in a circle. The rhythm is established of slapping thighs twice, clapping hands twice, snapping right fingers twice, then left fingers twice. When all are doing these motions in a good, strong rhythm, the first child calls out "A" as he snaps his right fingers, then gives a word beginning with A as he snaps his left fingers, keeping the rhythm going. Immediately, and in rhythm, the next child to the right calls the letter B on the right finger snap, and gives a word beginning with B on the left finger snap. The game continues around the circle in rhythm. It should be established before the game that the letter X will be skipped.

LANGUAGE ARTS ACTIVITIES

INDIVIDUAL SEATWORK

Correct the Teacher
The teacher writes a paragraph on the board, using incorrect spellings, punctuation, etc. The pupils copy the paragraph, correcting all the mistakes they can find.

Scrambles
Choosing sentences from current lessons in history, spelling, reading, or of timely interest, the teacher scrambles the word order in writing the sentences on the board. The pupils write the sentences in the correct order.

Similes
Using descriptive phrases as colorful and imaginative as possible, the children complete the sentence beginnings on the board, such as: "Happy as a _____"; "Silly as a _____"; "Fast as a _____"; "Dizzy as a _____."

Synonyms
Each pupil copies a paragraph from the board, or a designated paragraph in a book, and substitutes a synonym for every word that he can, using a dictionary.

Recipes
The class makes an "original recipe book" to be presented to the absent teacher on her return. Each child writes a description of how he would go about preparing his favorite food. The teacher should be sure that the children understand that the recipe is for fun and doesn't need to be accurate, also that spelling or punctuation will not be corrected.

Fantastic Animals

Each pupil draws a very imaginary animal and gives an oral or a written report on where it might be found, what it eats, its name, its habits, why no one has ever seen one, etc.

Story Writing

1. The children write a short story using dialogue between two things, such as one shoe talking to the other, two worms, dragons, newborn twins, Halloween ghosts, reindeer, snowflakes.
2. The children write about a gripe and how they would solve it.
3. The teacher puts sentence beginnings on the board to be developed into a written paragraph. Suggested sentence beginnings: "Mom, you won't believe this, but the reason I'm so late getting home from school is that . . ."; "Happiness is ..."; "If I were principal, I would ..."; "On the day I woke up and discovered I was invisible, I ..."

Mixed-up Storybook Tales

Storybook or nursery rhyme characters are used in different situations as the basis for short stories. Example titles: Snow White and the Seven Hippies, Goldilocks and the Three Surfers, Alice in Martian Land, Jack and the Watermelon, Aladdin and His Magic Yo-Yo.

Haiku

After a discussion on haiku and a few joint efforts by the class at writing it, the pupils make up their own. The first line must have five syllables; the second line, seven syllables; and the third line, five syllables. The use of descriptive words should be encouraged. Example:

> Soft wind of the night,
> Gently stirring leaves and grass,
> Soothe my troubled mind.

CLASS GAMES AND DRILLS

Spelling Password

The teacher chooses one child to be the guesser and one to be the writer. The guesser stands at the front of the room with his back to the board while the writer writes one of the spelling words from a current lesson on the board. Anyone in the class may raise his hand if he has a one-word clue to help the guesser determine which spelling word is written on the board behind him. For instance, if the written word is many, the clue may be lots. The guesser gets three clues, calling on anyone he wants, and three guesses to guess the word. If he succeeds, he gets another turn, and a new writer is chosen. The one-word clues may not be forms of the written word or contain it. After three wins, the guesser should choose someone to take his place. On guessing the word, the guesser must spell it correctly in order to stay up.

Descriptions

The teacher holds up a common object, such as an eraser, onion, ruler, plant, then asks the class to write descriptions of the object. After five minutes, the children turn their papers over. Now the teacher gives a short lesson on descriptions, emphasizing the use of the five senses. The class writes a second description of the same object, using as many adjectives, comparisons, and senses as possible. After about ten minutes, several pupils read their two descriptions aloud to see the improvements.

Dictation

The class is divided into two teams. One member from each team comes to the board and writes a sentence as the teacher dictates it. One point is given to the team whose member made the fewer number of errors.

Correct the Teacher

The teacher writes a paragraph on the board using misspellings and wrong punctuation and omitting punctuation. The pupils raise their hands to come to the board to correct one mistake. The activity continues until all the mistakes have been corrected.

Cinquains

The teacher discusses with the class what cinquains are and gives a few examples. Then the class creates an original one, which the teacher writes on the board. When the class is satisfied with the cinquain, each pupil copies and illustrates it. In a cinquain the first line has just one word, which should name the topic or theme of the poem. The second line is composed of two descriptive words, describing the subject. The third line has three words, expressing an action. The fourth line has four words, giving a feeling or a comparison. The last line is one word, a synonym of the first line.

Examples:

Spider	Rain
Tiny, creeping	Wet, fresh
Busy spinning webs	Helping flowers grow
More patiently than man	Refreshing all the land
Weaver	Showers

Adjectives

Two teams of five members each stand on opposite sides of the front of the class. The teacher gives the first member of Team 1 a noun. He must immediately give an appropriate adjective for this noun, then the next player on the same team gives a second word that logically describes the noun, and on down the line. A time limit is set within which the five team members must give their adjectives. If they succeed, score one point for that team, and go on to Team 2. Example: <u>Monkey</u>: hairy, funny, swinging, long-tailed, cute.

Spelling Bee

The class is divided into two teams. The first player on one team names any word of more than three letters and spells it aloud. The first member of the other team must immediately name a word, more than three letters long, which begins with the last letter of the first word spelled. This player then spells his word, and the second member of the first team then names a word beginning with the last letter of his opponent's word, etc. One point is awarded for each word that is given and spelled correctly, within the time limit.

Topic Sentences

The teacher reads aloud a paragraph from a social studies lesson, a science book, a news magazine, a newspaper, etc. The pupils then write one sentence, stating the main idea or the topic of the paragraph. Several pupils read their sentences aloud to compare. The topic sentences could be written in the form of a newspaper headline.

Silly Story

Three column headings are put on the board: Who, When, Where. The class gives words to be placed under each heading. For instance, under the Who column might be listed "Santa Claus," "Tiny Tim," "The man from Mars," "Three goblins," etc. Under When might be "The day the earth crumbled," "When the principal had the measles," "The day I become twenty-one," etc. The Where listing might contain phrases such as, "On the way to the moon," "In a cozy cottage," "Under the sea," "In a subway," etc. Each pupil then makes one selection from each column and uses the three items in an original story.

Spelling Baseball

The class is divided into two teams, and the teams line up on opposite sides of the room. One child is chosen to be the pitcher and sits at a desk in the center of the room, with a spelling word list in front of him. Three desks are designated as first, second, and third base, respectively. The first member of Team 1 comes center front as the batter, and the pitcher pronounces a word. In order to make a hit, the batter must spell the word correctly. If he does no, he may proceed to first base and the second player on the same team comes up to bat. If the second player also correctly spells his word, the first player moves to second base and the second player goes to first base. If a player misspells a word, it is an out for his team, and he goes to the end of his team's line. After Team 1 has three outs, its inning is ended, and Team 2 takes its turn at bat. A point is scored each time a player completes a move around the bases.

Spelling Game

On the board the teacher makes five rows of five dots each, evenly spaced about six inches apart. The class is divided into two teams. All remain seated while the teacher pronounces a spelling word for the first member of Team 1. If the player spells it correctly, he may come to the board and connect any two of the dots with a straight chalk line. The game continues, with turns alternating from Team 1 to Team 2. When a player forms a closed square by connecting two dots, he may put his team's number inside the square and he gets another turn. If a player misses a word, no dots are connected and the turn goes to the opposing team. The team who has its numeral in the most squares when all the dots are connected is the winning team.

MATH GAMES AND DRILLS

Number Memory

The pupils hold their pencils up while the teacher reads aloud a five-digit or six-digit number, then calls, "Begin." At this signal, the children write the number on their papers. The procedure is repeated until ten numbers have been read, after which the pupils exchange papers and check.

Math Bingo

The teacher prepares ahead of time sixteen math problems and their answers. These should be problems that the class can easily solve. Each child folds his paper into fourths each way, making sixteen squares. The teacher calls off the problem answers, which the pupils write in any square, at random, so that each paper will have the numbers in a different sequence. Each child will need markers, such as pieces of torn paper. The teacher then reads a problem and the children find and cover the answer on their papers. The first child to have four covered squares in a row calls out, "Bingo!"

Divide

The class can be asked to solve $987654312 \div 8$. Pupils may be surprised to find that the quotient is 123456789.

Speedy Addition

In this exercise the teacher can show the pupils how to add, or pretend to add, five numbers of as many digits as desired, arriving at the sum with unbelievable speed. First, the teacher writes a number on the board, perhaps using five digits. Then a pupil writes a number of his own choosing under the teacher's number. This, too, must be a five-digit number. Then the teacher writes the third number, pretending to do so at random, but actually "making nines," by putting down a number which, when added to the digit above it, will equal nine. The pupil then writes another five-digit number under the teacher's, and the teacher writes a fifth number, being sure that each digit she writes makes a nine when added to the digit above it. Then the teacher draws a line under the five numbers and immediately writes in the correct sum. The sum is always the top number, minus two, with a two in front of it, as shown. The pupils will delight in learning how to find this sum so that they can play the trick on their parents or friends.

```
Teacher writes
any number →      2 6 3 6
Pupil writes      4
any number →   6  1 8 2 4
Teacher →      3  8 1 7 5
makes nines
Pupil →        5  4 9 6 1
Teacher +      4  5 0 3 8
makes nines   _____
              2  4 2 6 3 4
              ↑            ↑
Always put a      same as top
2 here            number, less 2
```

44

Favorite Number

Another interesting exercise is to multiply the numeral 123456789 by any single digit, then multiply the product by 9. The answer, if the problem was done correctly, will contain no numeral except the first chosen single digit or 0.

Conductor

One pupil is chosen to be the conductor and stands beside the first desk in the first row and faces the teacher. The teacher flashes a card with a multiplication or division fact having a missing product or quotient. The conductor races the pupil beside whom he is standing to call out the answer. If the conductor gives the answer first, he moves to the next child in the row. If he is beaten, he sits down, and the one who beat him is the new conductor. In case of a tie, the teacher gives another problem.

Relaxer Movements, Pantomimes, and Discussion Openers

RELAXER MOVEMENTS

CONDITIONING EXERCISES

While seated

1. Stretch and bend as far as possible to the front, back, and each side. Repeat several times.
2. Stretch both arms overhead and make small circles, then larger ones, then reverse the direction of the motion.
3. Reach both arms out to the sides and make circular motions, first small, then larger, again reversing direction.
4. Pretend to be rowing a boat, stretching and tensing the arm muscles as the pulling motion is done.
5. Twist the head as far to the right, then as far to the left, as possible, while sitting straight and tall.

Standing beside desks

1. Place hands on the head, then the shoulders, then the knees, then the toes. Do this quite rapidly on the leader's command.
2. Jumping Jacks. Clap hands high over head and, on the same count, jump up, landing with feet apart. On the next count bring arms straight down to the sides while jumping and landing with feet together. Repeat.
3. Scissors Jump. Place hands on hips and jump, landing with one foot to the front and the other to the back. Alternate foot positions on each jump.
4. With hands on hips and feet close together, first slowly raise up on toes, then slowly bring heels down again.

5. Run in place, bringing knees up as high as possible.
6. Keeping feet in place, lean forward and make long, swimming strokes.
7. With hands on hips and feet firmly placed about a foot apart, twist the body at the waist to the right, then to the left.
8. Pretend to jump rope, jumping in place first with both feet together, then one foot at a time, alternating.
9. With feet apart and legs straight, touch right toe with left hand, stand straight, touch the left toe with the right hand and raise to a standing position, arms outstretched. Repeat.
10. Place hands on hips, feet a few inches apart. Keeping back straight up and down, bend at the knees into a squatting position, then raise up again. Repeat.

<u>Can You Do What I Do?</u>

This activity is especially good for calming down or relaxing younger children. The class sits in a circle Indian-style. The teacher reads the following poem slowly, doing the motions. Then the teacher asks the children to do the motions with her.

CAN YOU DO WHAT I DO?
Shut your eyes as tight as can be.
Squeeze them shut so you can't see.
Now open them wide and roll them around.
Look way up, and now way down.

Can you wiggle your chin?
Make your head sway?
Roll it around.
Now the other way.

Shrug your shoulders
Do it once more.
Now bend way down -
Can your head touch the floor?

Reach your arms out in front -
Stretch your very best.
Play you're rowing a boat.
Pull them back to your chest.

Put your hands on the floor
In back of you now.
Can you tip your head back?
Way back? Show me how.

Pretend you just woke
From a long, restful nap.
Stretch and stretch and stretch!
Lay your hands in your lap.
                M. L. M.

Horses Run

Everyone stands beside his desk, facing a leader. The leader calls out, "Horses run!" and runs in place. Everyone begins running in place. Then the leader names another animal, such as "Lions run!," and all continue to run in place. However, if the leader names something that cannot run, such as "Tables run!," the class should stop running in place, even though the leader continues his running. Anyone who fails to stop running when the object named is not one that runs must sit down.

Simon Says

When this game is played specifically as a relaxer, the teacher should be the leader, using bending, stretching, twisting, and jumping motions. The emphasis is more on getting the pupils "loosened up" than on tricking them into being "out." (See the section on indoor games for directions.)

PANTOMIMES

Children have a natural love of pretending. Through pantomime they are able to express themselves spontaneously and creatively. Since the teacher's role is that of guide rather than director, the children are able to experience growth in poise and cooperation without sacrificing individuality. Through the dramatic art of pantomime, pupils may experience speech and language improvement, more controlled emotional outlets, and growth in creative and imaginative expression.

Feelings

The teacher begins showing the children how to express themselves without words by having them pantomime the following feelings:

1. You are happy.
2. You are angry.
3. You are frightened.
4. You are excited.
5. You are hungry.
6. You are hot.
7. You are surprised.
8. You are sassy.
9. You are cold.
10. You are sleepy.
11. You are sulking.
12. You are wondering.
13. You are sad.
14. You are cheerful.
15. You are puzzled.
16. You are tired.
17. You are silly.
18. You are hurt.
19. You are suspicious.
20. You are bored.

Using the Whole Body

The teacher asks the children to use various body parts to relate a message.

1. Show with your head, "Yes."
2. Show with your eyes, "Help!"
3. Show with your ears, "I hear footsteps."
4. Show with your tongue, "This ice cream is delicious!"
5. Show with your nose, "This flower smells good."
6. Show with your shoulders, "I don't know."
7. Show with your eyebrows, "That makes me mad."
8. Show with your arms, "I'd better run fast."
9. Show with your finger, "Come here."
10. Show with your fingertips, "That's hot!"
11. Show with your legs, "I'm so tired of walking."
12. Show with your foot, "How much longer am I going to have to wait?"

Charades

Individual pupils pantomime actions while the rest of the class attempt to guess what the actions are. The children might make up their own actions, choose from this list, or draw slips of paper on which these ideas have been written. Clarity of action should be stressed.

1. Address and stamp an envelope.
2. Open a door, walk through, close, and lock the door.
3. Pick up and dial a telephone.
4. Fly a kite.
5. Get a drink of milk from the refrigerator.
6. Take a bath.
7. Be a barber.
8. Cut out a clipping from the paper.
9. Wash a window.
10. Be a policeman giving a ticket.

11. Be a fireman going to a fire.
12. Saddle a horse.
13. Hang clothes on the line in the wind.
14. Take socks out of a drawer, close the drawer, put on the socks.
15. Put paper in a typewriter and begin typing.
16. Sharpen a pencil.
17. Bounce a large ball.
18. Set the table.
19. Play a piano.
20. Thread a needle.
21. Slice a cake and eat a piece of it.
22. Pick up a pet - a cat.
23. Hang a picture on a wall.
24. Look through a microscope.
25. Unscrew a light bulb and put a new one in.
26. Cook hot cakes.
27. Wrap a gift.
28. Paint a wall.
29. Polish shoes.
30. Arrange a vase of flowers.
31. Eat a banana.
32. Lick an ice cream cone.
33. Make a sandwich.
34. Feed a goldfish, then watch it.
35. Make a campfire.
36. Pack a suitcase.
37. Make a phone call from a phone booth.
38. Be a woman getting ready for a dressy party.
39. Be a pitcher warming up.
40. Be a cowboy on a bucking horse.

Laughing

Several children are chosen for a laughing contest. Each one, in turn, faces the class, pretends to read a joke from a slip of paper, then begins laughing silently. The soundless laughs can build up from a chuckle to rolling on the floor, holding sides, and drying eyes. The actor who gets the most laughter from his audience is the winner.

Animals

As a pupil pantomimes an animal, the class trys to guess which animal is being portrayed.

1. cat (rub against something, lap milk, curl up)
2. dog (sit up, roll over, wag tail)
3. deer (run gracefully, head high and tilted)
4. monkey (swing by one arm, scratch, leap)
5. bull (snort, paw ground, charge)
6. hen (pretend to hatch an egg, flap wings)
7. gorilla (arms and legs curved outward, beat chest)
8. horse (gallop, prance, buck)
9. crocodile (swim, snap jaws)
10. bear (waddle slowly, give bear hug)
11. wolf (howl with chin high, creep up on something)
12. seal (swim, clap fins, balance ball on nose)
13. rabbit (hop, chomp imaginary carrot)
14. squirrel (crack nuts, jerky head motions)
15. goat (charge, butt)
16. kangaroo (squat and hop, hands held limply in front)
17. lion (roar, make swipes with claws)

Human Sounds

Several children must use exaggerated facial expressions and body movements to indicate a sound. The rest of the children try to identify the following sounds:

1.	shout	15.	sneeze
2.	snort	16.	hum
3.	blow	17.	cough
4.	laugh	18.	shriek
5.	cry	19.	whistle
6.	pant	20.	sigh
7.	gasp	21.	choke
8.	groan	22.	sing
9.	giggle	23.	gulp
10.	smack	24.	growl
11.	swallow	25.	breathe
12.	sputter	26.	chuckle
13.	whisper	27.	snarl
14.	sniff	28.	gurgle

Nursery Rhymes

A group of players act out, silently, a favorite nursery rhyme for the rest of the class to guess.

Jack Be Nimble	Jack Spratt
Little Miss Muffet	Mary Had a Little Lamb
Simple Simon	Old Mother Hubbard
Humpty-Dumpty	Rock-a-Bye, Baby
Little Boy Blue	There Was a Crooked Man
Old King Cole	Ring Around the Rosie
Mary, Mary, Quite Contrary	Pat-a-Cake
Pease-Porridge Hot	London Bridge
Little Jack Horner	Jack and Jill
Hey! Diddle, Diddle	Georgy Porgy
Rub-a-Dub-Dub	Diddle, Diddle, Dumpling
Little Bo-Peep	Jack Be Nimble
Three Blind Mice!	Sing a Song of Sixpence
To Market, To Market	Peter, Peter, Pumpkin Eater
One, Two, Buckle My Shoe	Ding, Dong, Bell

Sports

The children try to guess what game the performer is acting out. For variety, the pantomime can be done in slow motion.

1. football
2. bowling
3. archery
4. tennis
5. basketball
6. skating
7. badminton
8. broad jump
9. water ski
10. high jump
11. baseball
12. dodge ball
13. shot put
14. discus throw
15. dart throw
16. weight lifting
17. croquet
18. handball
19. pole vault
20. ice hockey
21. javelin throw
22. volley ball
23. skiing
24. hurdle race
25. sprint
26. table tennis
27. speedboat race
28. golf

DISCUSSION OPENERS

What Would You Do If ...?

For a change of pace from seatwork, or to fill in a few unscheduled minutes, the class is grouped in a comfortable arrangement conducive to conversation. The children are encouraged to be at ease, yet attentive, and considerate of the person whose turn it is to talk. The teacher tells the class that she is going to give them a pretend situation for them to think about, and to take turns talking about. She asks the class, "What would do do if ..." followed by one of these listed situations. The pupils silently think over the idea, then raise their hands if they would like to tell about what they would do. The teacher must try to get several ideas for each situation, and keep the discussion going by asking such questions as, "Why wouldn't that be a very good idea, Mary?" Or, "John, what would you do instead?" It is wise to go on to a new situation question before the children tire of the one being discussed.

1. ... you were alone in a rowboat in the middle of a small lake and the boat began to leak?
2. ... you were riding with a friend in his parents' car and your friend's father tossed a crumpled candy wrapper out of the window?
3. ... while walking down the street you saw smoke beginning to curl out from under a roof?
4. ... when camping with your family, you went to gather firewood and lost your way back to camp?
5. ... the couple who had been camping in the site next to yours loaded up their things and started to drive away, leaving their area littered, and their campfire burning?
6. ... when hiking in the hills about three miles from any house, your friend cuts his leg badly on some barbed wire?

7. ... the umpire called you "out," but you knew you had "tipped" the ball on that third strike?

8. ... you found out that a good friend of yours was taking things from stores without paying for them?

9. ... your best friend tried to talk you in to going swimming in a pond without asking your parents' permission?

10. ... your mother had asked you to watch your little brother for about an hour while she did some shopping, and she hadn't returned after three hours?

11. ... you saw a little boy who had climbed too high up into a tree and was crying, afraid to come down?

12. ... you were walking home and had a long way to go, when a nice-looking woman offered to give you a ride?

13. ... you saw the little boy next door playing with matches behind his garage?

14. ... a small, cute dog came up to you, wagging his tail and dragging a leash as though he were lost?

15. ... the new boy at school was sitting all alone at lunch hour, but your ball game was about to begin, and you were needed to play second base?

16. ... your little sister's piano recital happened to be on the same night as a birthday party you had been invited to?

17. ... your dad's birthday was tomorrow and you had no money?

18. ... you and a friend each received free passes to a one-day circus, then your friend became sick the day of the circus?

Topics for Individual Responses

The following titles or topics may be written on separate pieces of paper for the pupils to draw at random, or they can be written on the board so that the children can choose a subject of interest to them. It is hoped that these titles will inspire imaginative, creative stories or descriptions to be shared orally with the class. The pupils may write down their thoughts and ideas first, then read aloud the stories, or they can give their ideas orally, in an informal, impromptu way. The teacher may state one topic and ask three or four pupils to give their ideas on this one subject, for comparison of individual ideas.

1. What I Will Do when I Become Mayor
2. What I Would Do if I Were Principal
3. The Woman I Admire the Most and Why
4. The Day My Pet Deserved a Medal
5. Thoughts of a Newborn Baby
6. The Man I Most Admire and Why
7. How I Would End Pollution
8. The Ideal Means of Transportation
9. What I Would Order for a Favorite Feast
10. How I Escaped from the Cave-in
11. How I Would Spend a Thousand Dollars
12. My Excuse for Being Three Hours Late Getting Home from School
13. How I Became the Team's Hero
14. A Description of a Car's Engine
15. When the Lights Went Out in Our Submarine
16. How I Was Saved by a Mirror
17. When the Lion Escaped from Its Cage

18. How I Began the Morning in Weightless Space
19. What Happened the Night My Waterbed Sprang a Leak
20. The Time I Was Surrounded by Indians
21. How to Change a Tire
22. Why We Should Have a Children's Day
23. Why Exercise Is Important
24. Why I Decided to Come Home After Running Away
25. The Persons I Would Choose for Parents, Other than My Own Mom and Dad
26. A Description of Life on Mars
27. Five Things Our Town Has Better than Any Other Town
28. How I Would Improve Myself
29. Thoughts My Dog Has when I'm Teaching Him a New Trick
30. How I Would Prepare My Favorite Food
31. The Day I Got Up on the Wrong Side of the Bed and Did Everything the Opposite or Backward All Morning
32. The Time I Filled My Gas Balloon Too Full
33. You Wouldn't Believe What I Caught on My Fishing Pole
34. What Age in Time I Would Like to Live in and Why
35. What Real or Fictional Person I Would Like to Be
36. How Our School Could Be Improved

Games

INDOOR GAMES

<u>Doggy's Bone</u>

The children sit in a circle. One child sits in the center, head in lap, eyes closed and covered with his hands. Beside the child in the center is an object, such as an eraser, representing the doggy's bone. The teacher taps one of the children in the circle. This child quietly creeps up and takes the bone from beside the sleeping doggy and returns to his place in the circle, hiding the bone behind him. Each of the other pupils holds his hands behind his back, in order to fool the doggy. Before opening his eyes and looking up, the doggy asks, "Who has my bone?" The one who holds it answers, in a disguised voice, "Bowwow." The doggy then opens his eyes and has three guesses as to who has his bone. This game may be varied for special days. For example, in the fall the one in the middle could be the squirrel with a nut beside him; near Thanksgiving, there could be the farmer with his turkey; at Christmas, Santa and a toy; at Halloween, the witch and a cat. Appropriate sounds for these should be used.

Follow-the-Leader
   The class lines up behind a leader and follows him about the room, imitating the leader's motions. Before the game begins, the teacher may make several suggestions for motions, such as hands on the head, arms out to the side, walking on tiptoe, hopping, skipping, hands on hips, walking backward, leaning to one side, bending over at the waist.

Drop the Handkerchief
   This game may be played in the traditional way, with the runner dropping a seasonal object instead of a handkerchief on his way around the circle. A paper pumpkin, a jingle bell, a valentine, or a paper Easter egg could be used.

Detective
   A detective, a murderer, and a doorkeeper are chosen. The detective leaves the room. Then the murderer taps someone on the shoulder. The one who is tapped hides in a place previously determined by the teacher. Then all the children quietly change seats. The doorkeeper summons the detective to come back into the room. The detective has one minute and three guesses to figure out who is missing. If he succeeds, he may be the detective again. If he fails, he chooses someone to take his place. A new murderer is chosen each time. There is no need to change seats after the first move.

Eraser Tag

One child is chosen to be It and another to be the one chased. Each places an eraser (blackboard type) on his head and must walk about the room, with It attempting to tag the other player. The one being chased may, at any time, place his eraser on the head of any of his seated classmates. This new person then becomes It and must chase the former It. The one being chased is encouraged to place his eraser on another's head in a short time, so that several will get a chance to participate. If the players run, instead of walk, others are chosen to take their places.

Simon Says

The teacher or leader rapidly gives commands, usually preceded by "Simon says." Any command that is not preceded by "Simon says" should not be followed. Any player who moves to such a command must be seated. The leader tries to confuse the players by moving to each of the commands he gives, whether it is preceded by "Simon says" or not.

Memory

The teacher gathers five small objects and gives them to one of the children, instructing him to give one object to each of five other children, who then hold the objects behind their backs. Each child in the class holds his hands behind his back to further confuse the guesser. The child who distributed the objects closes his eyes and turns around three times. He then attempts to name each object and tell who is holding it.

Seven Up

Seven children stand at the front of the room. The other members of the class put their heads on their desk tops and close their eyes. The seven children then move quietly about the room. Each taps one classmate and returns to the front of the room. Those who have been tapped raise their hands so as not to be tapped by a second player. When all seven tappers have returned to the front, they turn as a group to each child with his hand raised and ask him by whom he thinks he was tapped. Those who guess correctly then trade places with those who tapped them.

Elimination

The teacher stands with back to the class and with face near the wall while the children quietly and slowly move about the room. When the teacher calls, "Stop," or blows a whistle, all must freeze where they are. Without turning around to look, the teacher then says something such as "the three nearest the center of the room." The teacher turns around to see who the three nearest the center of the room are, and these three must be seated. The game continues with such phrases as "the two nearest the flag," "the one nearest Billy," "the four nearest me," "the one nearest the fish tank," "the two nearest the pencil sharpener." When only a few children remain standing, the teacher eliminates one at a time. The last child standing is the winner.

I Spy

A small object is shown to the class. Then the children hide their eyes while the teacher places the object somewhere in the room in plain sight. It may be partly concealed, or in a place where one must stoop down, look around, etc. At the signal, "Go," the children move quietly about, searching for the object. If a child spies the object, he pretends not to have seen it and continues looking about for a short while. Then he comes to the teacher and whispers in her ear where the hiding place is, then takes his seat. The object of the game is to avoid being the last one seated. Stress that a player can fool the others by not coming to whisper to the teacher immediately after finding the object.

Echo

Three children are chosen to hide somewhere in the room, all in the same place, such as behind the teacher's desk, in a coatroom, behind a piano or a partition. The teacher tells these three which one of them is to be the echo, without the rest of the class hearing. Then one of the children in the classroom is picked to make a sound. This sound could be "Yoo-hoo," or "Merry Christmas," or "Gobble-gobble," or any appropriate greeting. The child who is to be the echo answers like an echo, using a disguised voice. Then the three hiders come out. The teacher asks the class, "How many think the echo was Mary?" and, "How many think it was Sue?" or "John?" The object is to see whether the majority of the class was fooled or was correct.

Find the Leader

Everyone is seated in a circle. One child is chosen to be It. It turns his back and covers his eyes while the teacher points to a child in the circle who will be the leader. This leader starts a motion, such as tapping his knees, and all follow by doing the same motion. Other motions that can be used are drumming fingertips, pulling ears, rocking the head back and forth, nodding, opening and clenching fists. It may now turn around and watch. Quite often the leader changes the motion, and the class also changes, following their leader. The object is for It to guess who the leader is, so the children are careful not to stare at the leader but follow his changing motions by watching out of the corner of their eyes. It has three guesses to say who the leader is. Then the leader becomes It.

Clap In

The teacher hides a designated object somewhere in the room while It shuts his eyes. The rest of the class sees the hiding place. Then It begins looking for the object. The class claps softly when It is not near the object, and louder as he nears it, clapping very loudly when he is quite close, until he finds it.

Poor Pussy

Someone chosen to be pussy goes up to a classmate who must stroke pussy's hair, saying, "Poor pussy," three times without smiling or laughing. Pussy meows after each "Poor pussy." If a player smiles or laughs while petting pussy, he takes pussy's place.

Concentration

The teacher taps one child (who stands, then sits again). The teacher points to another child, who taps the child that the teacher tapped (who stands, then sits again) and then taps a second child (who also stands, then sits again). The teacher points to still another child, who must tap the first child (the one who was tapped by the teacher), wait for him to stand and sit again, then tap the second child (who stands and sits), then add an additional child by tapping. Each time the teacher points to a player, this player must tap, in order, those previously tapped, these children standing and sitting at each tap. He must then add one child by tapping. When a player makes a mistake, he is out.

Hunter

The teacher chooses a hunter. The hunter wanders among the children saying, "I'm going hunting and I'm taking you and you and you," tapping three children. These three children get up and follow the hunter around the room until he suddenly turns to face them, saying, "Bang!" At this signal the three race to their seats. The last one to his seat must stand along the losers wall. Or, the first one to his seat becomes the new hunter.

OUTDOOR GAMES

Follow-the-Leader

This game may be played in the traditional way. The leader should be encouraged to change his motions and activities often. New leaders are chosen every few minutes, thus giving turns to those who may not often be found in leader roles.

Three Deep

A double circle is formed with all children facing the center. Each child in the inner circle will have another child behind him. A runner and a chaser are chosen. The runner begins running around the outside of the circle, with the chaser trying to catch him. The runner may go around the circle only twice, then must duck into the center of the circle, standing in front of a pair of children, which makes him safe. The child on the outside of the circle in this group of three now becomes the chaser and must try to tag the former chaser, who now becomes the runner.

Squirrels in the Trees

Partners hold hands, facing each other, to form trees. Each tree contains one other child, who is a squirrel. In addition, there is one extra squirrel outside the trees. When the teacher blows the whistle, the squirrels must all change trees, and the extra squirrel tries to duck into an empty tree, leaving another squirrel without a home. After several whistle blows the game can be stopped, allowing each squirrel to trade places with one of the children forming his tree. This can be done once more so that all have a chance to be squirrels.

Car Tag

The class is divided into four groups and each group is given the name of a car make. All in one group could be Fords, all in another group could be Chevys, etc. Each child must remember his car make. The class forms one large circle, mixing the groups so that all the Fords won't be next to each other, etc. The teacher blows a whistle and calls out loudly, "Chevy!" or any of the car names being used. All the children from that group step out of the circle and run to the right, trying to tag the runner in front of them. They may go only once around the circle and back into their original place in the circle. Anyone tagged must go to the center of the circle, which is the junk pile for wrecked cars. When about half of the children are in the center, a new game can be started. The teacher may call out two car names, such as "Chevys and Buicks!"

Midnight

The group lines up along a straight line. One child is picked to stand several yards away, facing the group. The line of children slowly begins to advance toward the one facing them, while asking, "What time is it?" The single player calls out any time he wishes, such as "Two o'clock!" When the line of players is fairly close to him, he may respond to the question by saying, "Midnight!" which is the signal for the line to turn and run back to the original starting line, where the players become safe. Anyone caught by the one out front is on his side and helps catch others the next time, until all are caught.

Mousetrap

Three small circles are formed, each made up of three children holding hands. These three mousetraps are placed some distance apart about the play area. The rest of the children line up behind a leader, who leads them under the arms and through each mousetrap in turn, continuing in and out one after the other. On the teacher's whistle signal, the line must stop. Anyone caught within a mousetrap takes his place as a part of that trap by joining hands with the three, forming a circle of four. When the teacher calls, "Go," the line moves on again. As the mousetraps grow larger, several children can be caught at one time. The winner is the last one remaining out of the traps.

Dodge Ball

A large circle is formed, with several children inside the circle. Those children forming the circle attempt to hit the ones in the center with a large, soft ball. They must throw the ball low so that it hits below the waist in order to put a child out. When hit, the child in the middle must take a place in the circle and receive the ball for the next throw. A variation is to have only five or six children in the middle. If one of these children is hit with the ball, he trades places with the one who threw the ball, so that there are always the same number of children in the center. If two are hit on one throw, the first one hit trades places with the thrower.

Relay Ideas
1. Jump the Ditch. Halfway between each team and its goal line parallel lines are chalked in about two feet apart to be the ditch. The runners from each team must jump over their ditch and continue on to the goal line, then run back, jumping the ditch again.

2. A circle is marked at each team's goal line. One item, such as an eraser, a rock, or a twig, is put in each circle. The first runner from each team runs to the circle, picks up the object, and brings it to the second runner, who takes it back and puts it in the circle again. The third runner runs to the circle, picks up the object, and brings it to the fourth runner, etc.

3. The Ball Pass relay doesn't involve running. The first player on each team is given a ball. This player passes the ball over his head to the player behind him, who passes the ball under his legs to the player behind him. The players continue passing the ball alternately over and under. The team that first gets its ball to the last player in its row is the winning team.

4. The first player on each team stands on the goal line, facing the team. Each team has a ball. At the signal to go, the second player on each team carries the ball to a line marked halfway between the team and the goal line, stops, and throws the ball to his teammate on the goal line. That player catches the ball, runs, and gives it to the third person (now at the head of the line), while the one who threw the ball goes to the goal line to be the next catcher.

Call Ball

The class forms a large circle with one player in the center having a ball. This player throws the ball straight up as high as he can and calls out the name of one of the players in the circle. The child named attempts to catch the ball after it has bounced once. If he succeeds, he takes the ball to the center and becomes the one who throws it straight up while calling out another name. Children could be given numbers so that the caller would shout out a number rather than a name. This might discourage friends from calling their friends' names.

Catch

The class is divided into teams of eight or so. Each team lines up in a shallow semicircle, facing one of their team members, the thrower, who is standing about eight feet away and holding a ball. At the signal to go, the thrower throws the ball to the first member of his team, who catches the ball and throws it back. The thrower then throws to each team member in turn. When the last team member receives the ball, he takes the thrower's place in front of the team, and the former thrower becomes number one in his team's line. The first team to have all of its members complete a turn at being the thrower is the winning team.

Arts and Crafts

SIMPLE IDEAS FOR YOUNGER CHILDREN,
GRADUATING TO MORE COMPLEX FOR OLDER CHILDREN

Hand Trace

Trace around your hands, placed palms down on a sheet of paper, with fingers spread apart. Make several overlapping hand traces, then color in each space formed by the lines, making an allover pattern.

Crayon Resist

Color any design or picture heavily with wax crayons, leaving some of the paper showing. Using broad, straight strokes, paint over the entire piece of paper with black ink or tempera. The ink or paint will not adhere to the colored areas.

Blot Design

Fold paper in half, open it, and drop one drop of paint onto the center of the fold. Carefully refold the paper, then gently push, with fingertips, the drop of paint toward the edges of the paper. Open the paper and let the irregularly shaped blot dry. Trace around the outer edges of the blot with crayon. Now

trace around this crayon color with another color, and continue until the entire piece of paper has been filled.

Scrap Design

This is a good way to use up small scraps of colored paper. Paste irregularly shaped and variously colored scraps of paper onto black construction paper in a balanced design. Using a dry-brush technique (very little black paint on a wide brush), stroke downward from the top of the black paper to the bottom, tying the design together with the fine, black streaks.

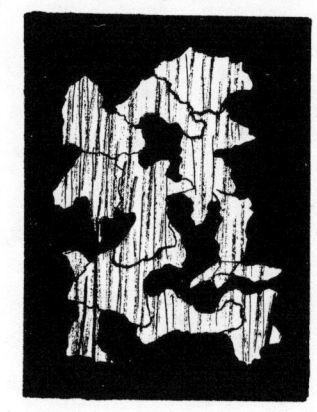

Fantastic Animals

Use your imagination to create a most fantastic animal, a combination of other animals you know, plus polka dots, unusual colors, etc. It is fun to give a name to your animal, and perhaps describe it to the class.

Wrinkle Design

Crumple or fold a piece of paper at various angles, then open it and color in the spaces formed by the creases in the paper. Outline these colored spaces with black crayon or felt-tip pen or by gluing on black yarn or string.

Chalk Painting

Mix some very thick white tempera. It should be thick enough to form peaks. Use this paint to block in a picture or a design on a dark-colored piece of construction paper. While the paint is wet, color into it with colored chalk. Use a circular motion, and leave some of the white of the paint showing. If a vase of flowers is being done, it works best to have several children at a time place the white paint where the flowers are to be, take their seats and work the colored chalk into these, then come back to the paint table to apply paint for the vase. This way the paint doesn't dry too fast.

Sunset Sky

Paint, or color with the flat, long side of crayons, wide, blending strokes of red, orange, and yellow. Cover the entire piece of paper smoothly, with horizontal strokes, to resemble a sunset sky. Now cut out scenes from black construction paper and paste them onto the colored paper as a silhouette. This is effective as a burned forest (during Fire Prevention Week), wheat sheaves, scarecrow and pumpkins, palm trees and sailboats, etc.

Rainbow Sky

Do this in the same manner as the above, but use rainbow colors and arched strokes. Silhouettes might be of flowers, bunnies, pine trees, mountain cabin, city building, etc.

Faces

This is a lesson on the basic principles of drawing faces. Begin with an oval shape. Place the eyes halfway between the top and the bottom of the oval. Place the mouth halfway between the eyes and the chin. Draw the top of the

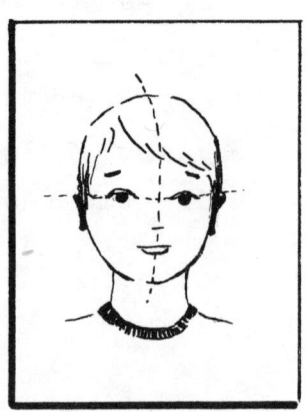

ears even with the eyes. Each child can draw himself and put his name on the back of the picture. The teacher collects the pictures and holds them up before the class. It is fun for the children to see how many portraits they can identify.

Initial Design

Make very large initials touching the edge of the paper and each other. Color in each of the spaces formed, then outline the initials with a heavy black crayon or felt-tip pen. The spaces could be filled with a pattern such as checks, plaids, dots, stripes, zigzag lines, or any the children think of.

Ladybugs

Use a yellow and an orange circle cut from construction paper. (The older classes can cut their own.) Cut the orange circle in half and arrange the half circles like wings on the yellow circle body. Cut out and paste on it the black head, feelers, legs, and dots.

Inside-out Design

Use one whole sheet of colored construction paper and one half sheet of a contrasting color. Cut irregular shapes from the sides of the smaller sheet, one shape from the shorter side and two shapes from the longer side. Paste the half sheet onto the center of the large sheet, then paste the cutout shapes along the edges to look as though they had been folded back from the edges.

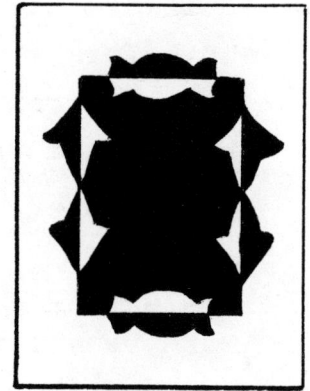

Jigsaw Art

Cut out a simple shape (tree, animal, bell, bottle, car, plane, fruit, ghost for Halloween, heart for Valentine's Day, etc.). Now cut this shape into several jigsaw shapes. Paste these onto a piece of contrasting-color construction paper in the original shape, but leave one fourth of an inch of space between the pieces.

Perspective

This is a basic lesson on perspective. Make two pencil dots, one on each side edge of the paper about halfway up, to represent the horizon level. Draw a vertical line on the paper, making sure that the top of this line is above the horizon level and the bottom of the line is below the horizon level. Then make light dashed lines from the top of this vertical line to the horizon dots and from the bottom of the vertical line to the horizon dots. Draw two more vertical lines, one on each side of the original vertical line, between the dashed lines, to represent the sides of the building, block, or box being drawn. Then make the dashed lines solid between the vertical lines, and erase the remaining dashed lines. Windows, doors, etc., can be added as long as all lines drawn are either vertical lines or lines going from the ends of vertical lines toward the horizon dots.

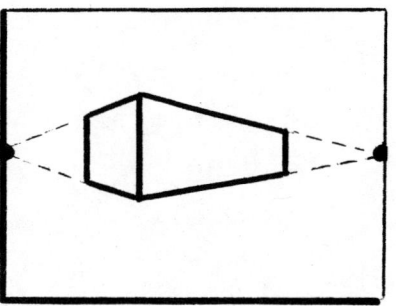

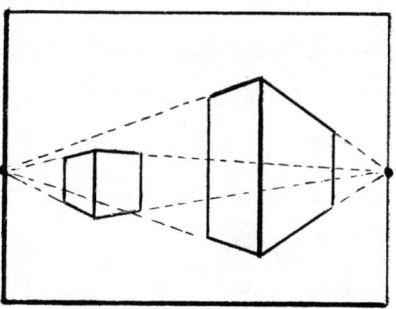

Name Design

Use typing or ditto paper, with large-squared paper underneath and showing through; or lightly mark off paper into one-inch squares. Print your first name, placing one letter in each square and making the letter as large as the square. Repeat the name, leaving no empty squares, using the whole paper. If each letter is repeated in its same color, a design will show up.

Paper-Strip Art

Cut many paper strips about 3/4 of an inch wide, some 12 inches long and some 6 inches long. Staple three 12-inch strips with the two outer strips forming a loop, as shown, for the basic form. Fill in the hoop with symmetrical curls, crosspieces, and loops made from the 6-inch pieces. The 12-inch strips may also be stapled to form birds, fish, etc. Use these designs as mobiles or hang them in windows.

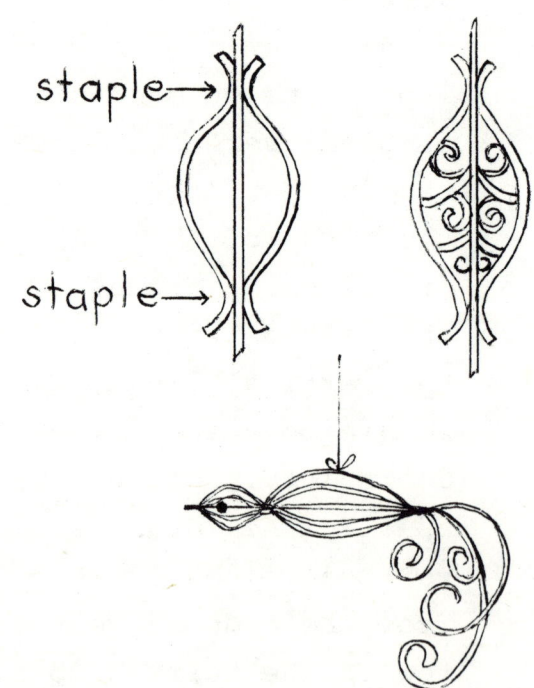

Name Trace

Write your first name with very dark crayon or felt-tip pen, making it as large as possible. Trace around this name, following the letters closely and carefully with a color crayon. Completely surround the original lettering with the color. Repeat, using another color, until the paper is entirely filled.

Name Design

Fold your paper lengthwise, then open it and write your name with crayon along the fold line, with each letter touching the fold but not going below it. Refold the paper and trace over where the name is written inside. This should leave an impression of the name on the other side of the fold as a mirrored image. Go over this impression with crayon, then color in the spaces formed, to make an interesting design. Mount the paper and display it vertically to show the design better.

Contrasts

Use a 9-inch by 12-inch sheet of colored construction paper and a 4½-inch by 12-inch piece of a contrasting color. Fold the smaller piece in half lengthwise and cut three or four irregular shapes from the folded side, beginning and ending the cut on the fold. Then unfold and paste the 4½-inch-wide piece onto the left half of the larger sheet, edges together. Find the cutout piece matching the shape nearest the top and, keeping it folded, cut another irregular shape from it. Now unfold and paste the larger cutout piece, directly across from its matching shape on the large sheet of paper. Paste the smaller cutout piece from this same shape in the center of the space opposite, so that a contrasting, symmetrical design is formed. Repeat for the other two or three shapes.

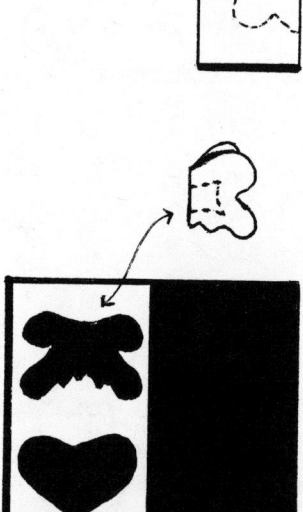

Symmetrical Design

Fold two pieces of 4½-inch by 6-inch lightweight paper into fourths. Cut an irregular shape from the corner that is bound by folds, beginning the cut on one folded edge and ending on the other folded edge. Open the papers and remove the cutout pieces. Use these four pieces to form a symmetrical design when they are pasted on a piece of colored construction paper. Try using brightly colored magazine illustrations, gift wrapping, or yardage for the cutouts.

Magic Cuts

Fold lightweight paper into thirds lengthwise, accordion fashion. Cut slits 1 inch apart from one folded edge to within 1 inch of the opposite edge. Now cut slits from the opposite folded edge to within 1 inch of the side, cutting between the first slits, so that all cuts will then be 1/2 inch apart. Open the paper, and holding one short end, gently pull the other short end. Hang the resulting design as a mobile, or use it as a background for bulletins.

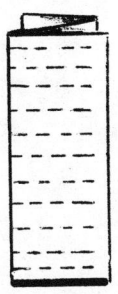

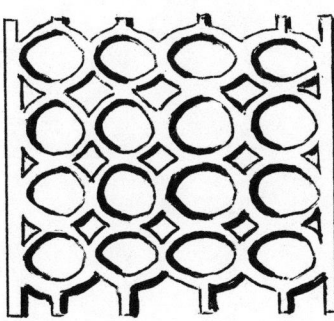

(The following arts and crafts ideas require some preparation.)

Straw Blow

Drop one small drop of watercolor or thin tempera onto a sheet of paper. Hold the straw at a slant toward the drop and very close to it. "Chase" the paint around on the paper by blowing, until the drop has been completely spread out into streaks and there is no wetness left. This is effective with one or two colors. The use of black paint on white paper, cut narrow and mounted on black, is quite striking.

Thumb Things

Rub oil pastel or colored chalk on your thumbs and make thumbprints on a small piece of paper. With a felt-tip pen, add details to suggest mice, owls, birds, fish, or anything you might think of.

Paper Plate Weave

Poke a hole in the center of a paper plate and nineteen holes about 3/4 of an inch from the rim. Make another row of holes about an inch toward the center from the first row, placing each hole midway between those in the outer row. Work yarn from the center hole to each hole in the inner circle, and another color of yarn connecting the two circles of holes. These spokes serve as a loom to weave in and out and around, forming any creative design.

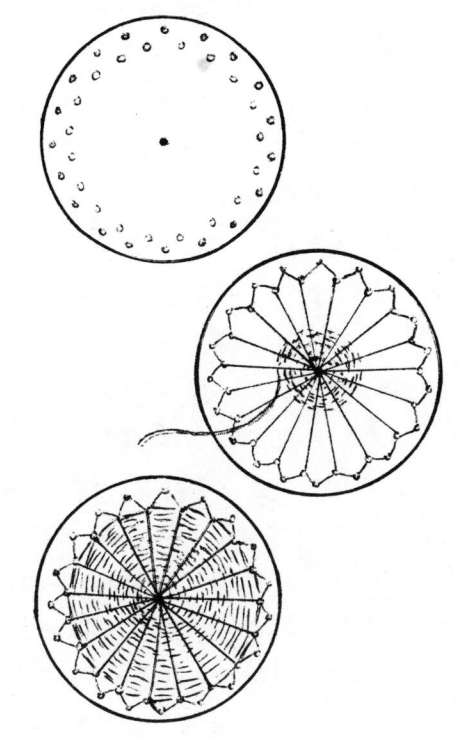

String Painting

Fold a piece of light-colored or white paper in half. Paint a piece of string with watercolor, rather dryly. Open the paper and carefully lay the wet string on one half of the paper in a wiggly pattern. Refold the paper, and pressing the paper with one hand, slowly draw the string out. When placing the string on the paper, leave one end free below the edge of the paper. The opened paper should reveal an interesting design.

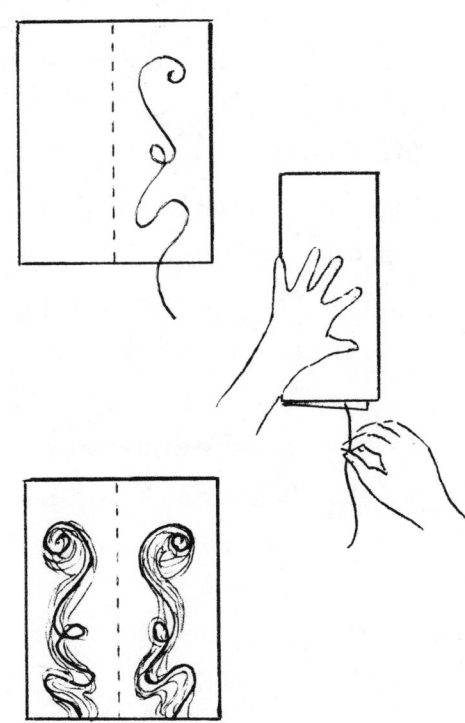

Wax-Paper Transparencies

Using very small dabs of glue, arrange overlapping shapes of varied colors of tissue on a sheet of wax paper. Shapes may be abstract or of flowers, birds, etc. Bits of yarn, thread, dried leaves, weeds, or flowers may be added. Cover the design with another piece of wax paper and press with a warm iron. A piece of newsprint will protect the iron from the wax. This can be done with bits of shaved crayon between the wax paper instead of (or in addition to) the paper, thread, dried weeds, etc.

Flat Papier-Mâché

Cut a butterfly shape from several layers of newspaper. Coat each shape with diluted white glue and stack them together. Let dry until they are stiff enough to hold a shape. Shape the wings into a natural position. When the butterfly is dry, paint it with tempera and then shellac. Add pipe-cleaner antennae and a pin on the back. Use a circle shape to form a pin dish.

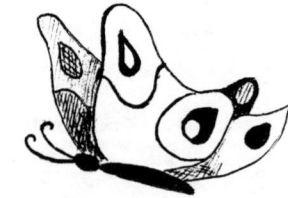

Macaroni Frame

Use a heavy paper plate or platter. Glue various types of macaroni around the rim in an even design. Spread a thin coating of glue on the rest of the plate and cover it with sawdust for a textured effect. Shake off the excess sawdust. Center an artificial flower or sprig of greenery and sew it on with heavy thread and a yarn needle. Spray completely with gold. Glue a hanger onto the back.

Beads

Cut 1-inch by 2-inch triangles from colored magazine illustrations and, beginning at the 1-inch end, roll each triangle tightly around a nail. Glue the point down and remove the nail. When enough beads are made, shellac and string them for necklaces, bracelets, key chains, or belts.

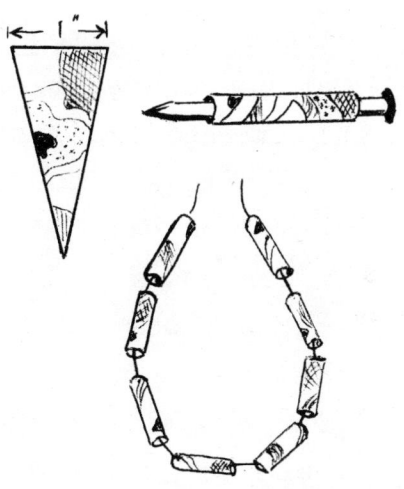

Papier-Mâché

Soak torn bits of newspaper in water overnight. Rub to a pulp and squeeze out the water. Add one cup of water to three cups of pulp and one-third cup of salt. Form into dishes, beads, masks, animals, puppet heads, relief maps, etc. Another method is to use crumpled paper, cardboard tubes, or balloons to form the papier-mâché over. The papier-mâché can also be made by dipping strips of newspaper into a wallpaper paste and applying them to a form. Making the last layer with paper toweling is a good idea if the object is to be painted.

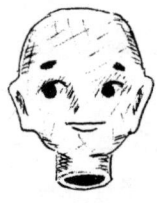

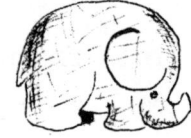

Magazine Illustration Collage

Cut up colored magazine illustrations into small shapes and glue them onto a piece of construction paper, or cardboard, overlapping the pieces and forming a picture or an abstract design. Try using all analogous colors, or cut out pictures all of one subject, using these to form a design relating to this subject (e.g., all pieces from floral pictures, pasted on in the shape of one large flower).

Lanterns

Accordion-pleat a piece of construction paper and cut notches from the edges. Open the paper and line it with a piece of tissue paper or cellophane the same size. Form this into a cylinder and hang several in groups in front of windows.

Cloth Flowers

Use colorful printed yardage scraps from which to cut out flower shapes. Use a solid-green material for leaves. Cut a flowerpot shape from burlap or any coarse, solid-colored material. Glue these shapes into a pleasing flower arrangement on a piece of construction paper.

Sponge Painting (pattern on page 127)

With a small piece of sponge dipped in paint and applied lightly to a piece of paper with easy dabs, many interesting effects are discovered. With pink paint, daub spring blossoms onto a previously drawn tree, or use fall colors for autumn foliage. Blue spongings make an ocean; white spongings make fluffy clouds or snow; etc.

Rock Sculpture

Use three or four small, smooth rocks. Glue them together in imaginative shapes of animals, people, planes, or whatever you like. Paint on details with acrylic paint. Spray the finished object with a plastic spray, or shellac.

"Me" Collage

Look through magazines and cut out pictures or words that are descriptive of yourself and your interests. Arrange and glue these in an overlapping design, to cover the paper completely. For instance, a peace-loving and nature-loving pupil might cut out and paste on pictures of the out-of-doors, quiet scenes, words such as "peace," "love," "Be kind," "sunshine," and perhaps he might find a picture of a dove, a sunset, a mother and child, etc.

Bread Dough

Mix together four cups of flour, one cup of salt, two tablespoons of vinegar, and one and a half scant cups of water. Knead thoroughly. Form into the desired shapes, or roll out to a half-inch thickness and cut out shape. Bake at 300° for one and a half to six hours, depending on the thickness of the object. When the objects are a light toast color, they should be done. Paint them with acrylic paint, then spray them with an acrylic or resin spray.

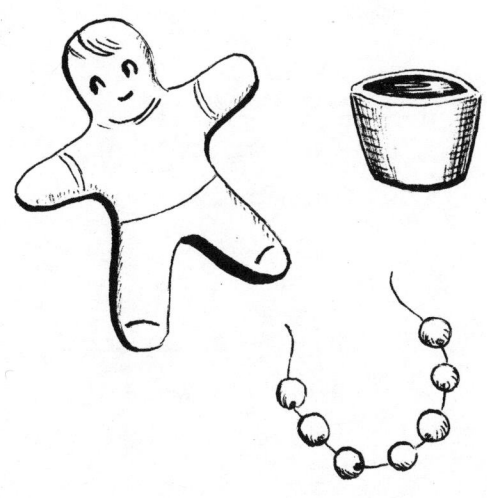

Yarn Names

Soak a piece of rug yarn 2 or 3 feet long in white glue, slightly diluted. "Write" first names on wax paper with the yarn and let dry. Spray with a clear plastic spray. When the names are dry, remove them from the wax paper and glue them to notebooks, pin them onto bulletin boards, or put them any place desired.

Bleached Highlights

Sketch a simple object on colored construction paper. Using a toothpick tipped with cotton and dipped in bleach, brush onto the picture where the light would hit the objects, making white highlights. Go over the rest of the sketch outlines with a felt-tip pen or black crayon. Shade areas away from the light source.

SEASONAL ARTS AND CRAFTS, INCLUDING HOLIDAYS

AUTUMN

Simple Tree

Cut or tear a large, rounded, orange shape from construction paper. Paste this onto a piece of blue or yellow background paper. Using a brush, piece of sponge, or wadded bit of paper toweling, daub yellow, brown, and green paint on the orange shape, for autumn leaf coloring.

Sponge Trees (pattern on page 127)

Cut out a dark-brown tree trunk and bare branches shape and paste it onto a piece of light-colored construction paper. Or, color the tree trunk and branches heavily with dark-brown crayon. Use a piece of sponge to daub on colors of paint to resemble fall foliage.

Torn-Paper Leaves (pattern on page 127)

Cut out or color a tree shape. Paste on torn bits of tissue or construction paper of fall colors for leaves. Scraps of appropriately colored magazine illustrations might be used.

Batik Leaves (patterns on page 128)

On a piece of construction paper, color heavy layers of fall colors, using wax crayons. Cover the entire paper with black paint or ink. Scrape off where a leaf shape is desired, letting the autumn colors show through. Paint or ink in the stem and veins.

Autumn Sky

Blend horizontal strips of red, orange, and yellow across all of a sheet of paper with paint, the side of a crayon, or colored chalk. Cut a bare-branched tree shape from black construction paper and paste it onto the colored paper. Add a few leaves in fall colors, some dropping to the ground.

Leaf Rub (patterns on page 128)

Cut out several varied leaf shapes from oak tag or heavy paper. Place a few of these at random under a sheet of lightweight paper and rub the side of a crayon in even strokes over the paper. Use autumn colors. Leaf shapes will appear where the crayon hits the edges of the cutout patterns.

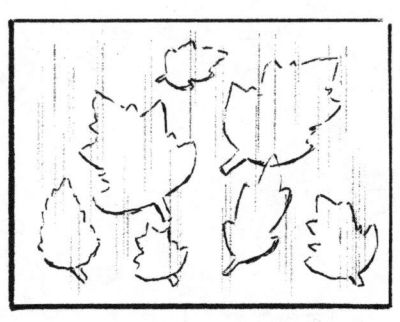

Leaf Men (patterns on pages 129, 130, 131)

Ditto leaf shapes, similar to those shown, onto manila paper. Color one of each in fall colors. The head is an acorn shape. Cut out the shapes and glue or staple them in the form of a leaf man. If both sides are colored, this may be used as a mobile.

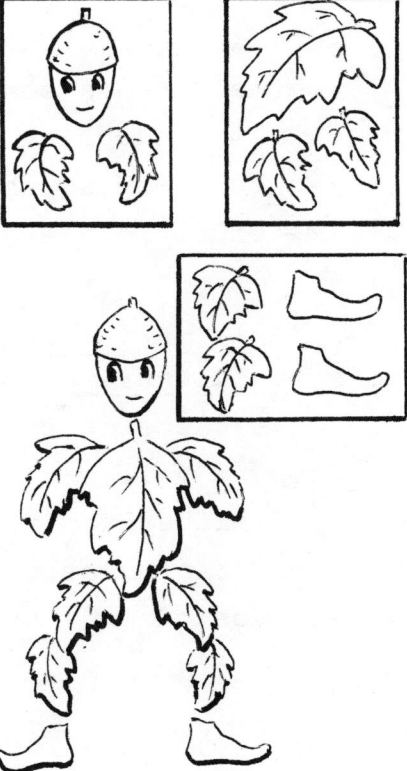

93

Chrysanthemums

Curl ½-inch by 3-inch strips of yellow or orange paper and paste the curls in several overlapping rows in a circle, to form a blossom. The strips should curl inward, toward the center of the flower. From green paper, cut out a stem and leaves and paste them in place. Use one half of a 9-inch by 12-inch piece of construction paper, cut the long way, to make a good backing for this flower.

Mobile Leaves

Staple one end of three 12-inch by ½-inch strips of construction paper, of fall colors. Slide the two outer strips up a few inches and staple to the center strip, forming a leaf shape. Fill in between these strips with short strips in curls, loops, and swags, keeping the leaf symmetrical in design.

Poem to Illustrate

On a piece of construction paper copy a fall poem from the board and illustrate it by pasting a border of overlapping, cutout leaves.

FALL HOLIDAY IDEAS

Columbus Day Ship
   Entirely cover a sheet of blue construction paper with blending strips of wavy crayoned lines in greens and blues and white, suggesting the sea. On this, paste a cutout picture of a ship such as the one in which Columbus sailed.

Stand-up Ship (pattern on page 132)
   Color a piece of blue construction paper with strips of greens, blues, and white, then accordion-pleat it to represent the ocean waves. Make a slit about 4 to 6 inches long across the folds in the center of the accordion pleats to hold a cutout ship. Make a large cloud behind the ship to save cutting around the sails and masts. This ship could be dittoed on manila paper for the children to color and cut out.

Free-form Pumpkin Head

Cut any imaginative free-form shape from orange paper and paste it onto black paper. Add green and yellow cutouts for stem, eyes, nose, and mouth.

Torn-Paper Ghost

Tear out a ghostly shape from white paper and paste it onto a light-blue paper background. Dark-blue or black background paper could also be used. Add eyes, trees, fences, bats, haunted houses, etc., with black crayon, if light-blue background is used, and with white chalk or crayon if dark-blue or black background is used.

Three-dimensional Faces

Cut out orange pumpkin heads. From white paper, cut out features. Color in pupils of eyes, teeth, etc. Use links made from paper strips to paste between the pumpkin face and the features to make them stand out.

Scissors Owls

Trace around a pair of scissors to make the outlines of owls. Add eye pupils, beaks, feathers, branches, moon, etc. This could be done on blue paper or on white, with the sky colored in.

Ghost Scribble

Make a continuous, curvy, scribble line on white paper. Find ghost shapes and add eyes. Color all spaces. This is an abstract design.

Etched Ghosts

Color random sections of construction paper heavily with various bright colors. Paint over the entire paper with black paint mixed with a little detergent. When this is dry, scratch a design or scene with a sharp point such as a bobby pin or the end of a paper clip.

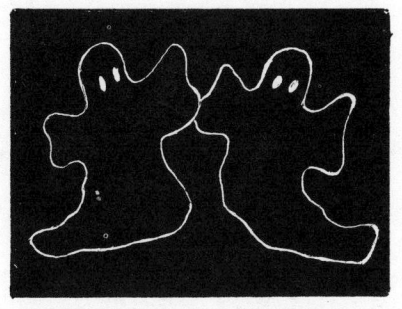

Overall Ghost Pattern

Heavily crayon ghosts in orange outlines, overlapping each other. Put a black watercolor or poster paint wash over all. Since the crayon will resist the black paint, the orange will show through.

Black Cats

Make two cylinders from black paper, one from a 10-inch by 4½-inch piece and the other from a piece 10 inches by 3 inches. Glue together to form a cat's body and head. Glue on orange eyes, nose, and feet, and black ears, whiskers, and tail.

Soda Straw Skeletons

Arrange pieces of cut-up straws for the bones of a skeleton. Glue these onto black paper. Make a skull-shaped head from white paper. Make the skeletons in various positions (dancing, leaping, etc.).

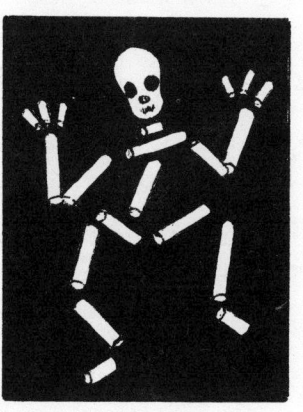

Facial-Tissue Ghosts

Use two tissues, a rubber band, and a piece of blue paper, 9 inches by 12 inches for each ghost. Roll and wad up one tissue for the head stuffing. Use the other tissue to place around and over this stuffing. Put the rubber band around the neck. Mark eyes on this ghost with a black felt-tip pen or crayon. Glue ghosts to the construction paper and color in the rest of a scene, such as fences, trees, bats, headstones.

Doily Face

Color a piece of lightweight paper orange. Fold it into fourths and cut notches and curved shapes on the folds. Open it and paste it onto a piece of black paper. Add white triangles for the eyes and nose, with smaller green triangles for pupils, and yet smaller black triangles inside the green. Cut a white mouth shape and paste an irregularly shaped black strip down the center of this white mouth.

Spiral Ghosts (pattern on page 135)

Use a ditto of a ghost shape, as shown. Or, the ghost could be drawn on the board and copied. Cut on the lines, causing the bottom of the ghost to spiral downward when it is hung. Add black eyes.

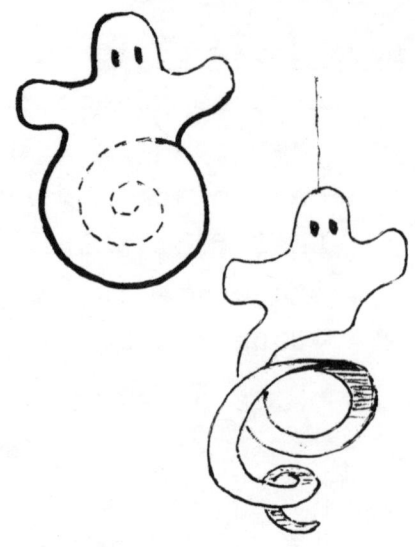

Spiral-tailed Mobile (pattern on page 136)
Cut out a black cat shape as shown. Paste on orange eyes, nose, and whiskers. Cut a spiral tail from an orange circle slit in a spiral. Hang the cat so that the tail drops downward.

Offset Ghost
Use an orange crayon and two pieces of 12-inch by 4½-inch construction paper, one black and one white. With scissors or by tearing, scallop the outer edges of the white paper. Carefully cut out a ghost shape from the center of the white paper, keeping the cutout part and the background part intact, as both will be used. Color the white background piece orange, and outline the white ghost with orange. Add black eyes to the ghost. Paste the scalloped orange piece onto the black paper, then paste the ghost at a slightly offset position.

Three-dimensional Witch Face
Cut out an orange circle and slit it to the center. Overlap the ends slightly at the slit, and glue them down, making a very shallow cone shape. Add a hat, eyes, nose, and mouth cut from black paper. Glue on strips of newspaper for hair.

Paper-Strip Pumpkin

Fasten several narrow strips of orange-colored paper together at one end, with a staple or a brad. Use at least ten strips. Spread these strips like spokes, then bring the ends together and fasten them, forming a round shape. Glue on black-paper features and a green stem.

Stand-up Witch

Cut a triangle 12 inches tall from along the side of a piece of black construction paper. It should have a slightly curved lower edge. Cut half-circle arms, about 4 inches across, and a 3-inch circle from the rest of the sheet of black paper. Cut a 3/4-inch triangle from the center of the circle. From orange-colored paper, cut a face shape about 1½ inches across the forehead, and cut two hand shapes. Decorations for the witch's dress can also be cut from the orange paper. Draw the witch's features with a black felt-tip pen or crayon. Paste the face onto the black triangle so that the edges of the face just touch the sides of the triangle. Paste the hands onto the ends of the arms, and the decorations along the bottom of the triangle. Slightly roll the triangle and slip the black circle onto the point of the triangle, working it down even with the witch's face. Two slits in the inner edges of the arms slip over the edges of the triangle and help to hold it in a curve. Add paper or yarn hair.

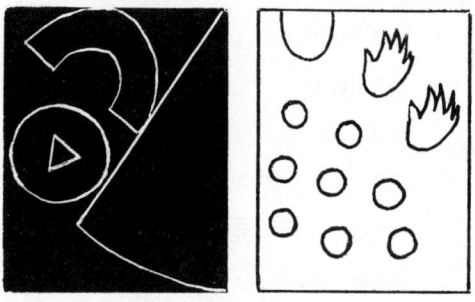

Stand-up Cat

Fold a 9-inch by 4½-inch piece of black construction paper in half width-wise and cut out a cat's body shape, as shown. Cut out the front legs shape from the front piece only. Accordion-pleat a black strip ½ inch by 4 inches for the tail, and paste to the middle of the back. Tape or glue an accordion-pleated neck to the top of the body. The neck strip should be about 1 inch wide by 4 inches long. To the other end of the neck, glue a head shape that has been decorated with white eyes (with orange centers), orange nose, and whiskers. The bottom illustration shows another version of a stand-up cat, put together in a similar manner.

Owl Mosaic

For this purpose a very simple outline can be dittoed, showing owl, branch, and moon. Using glue, fill in the body with dry oats, the moon with cornmeal, the sky with farina, and the branch with wheat germ or the like. Use rice for claws, Cheerios for eyes, and a clove for the beak.

Poem to Illustrate

HALLOWEEN

Witches soaring on
Their brooms,
Haunted house with
Ghost-filled rooms

    Can't scare <u>me</u> tonight!
    (Well ... maybe just a <u>mite</u>.)

Swarms of bats
In the night,
Jack-o'-lanterns'
Flickering light

    Don't even make me blink!
    (For I'm quite brave ... I <u>think</u>.)

Black cats' glowing
Yellow eyes,
Goblins' screechy,
Scary cries

    I'm not afraid of such!
    (At least ... not <u>very</u> much.)

        M. L. M.

Giant Turkey (pattern on page 137)

The teacher draws a large turkey's body, with no tail, on an 18-inch by 24-inch piece of construction paper, or on a piece of rolled wrapping paper. This is then tacked up on a wall. Each child traces around his hand on a piece of brown, orange, red, or yellow paper and cuts out the shape. These hand shapes are fastened to the large turkey, fingers pointing away from the body, overlapping, to resemble tail feathers.

Leaf-Tail Turkey (pattern on page 137)

On a piece of paper, draw a turkey body with no tail. Color this, then paste real leaves of various shapes and colors for the turkey's tail.

Three-dimensional Tepees

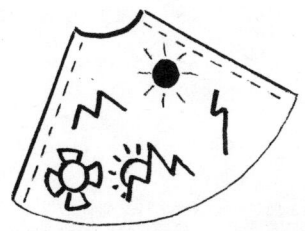

Color or paint a background scene of sky, trees, shrubs, and ground on white construction paper. Cut out a tepee shape (one fourth of a circle). Decorate the tepee with Indian symbol designs. Fold back a tab along each edge of the tepee. Make a slit for a door and fold open. Glue the tepee to the background scene by pasting the tabs, forming a cone shape. Tape small twigs to the top of the tepee.

103

Folded-Paper Turkey

Cut an 8½-by-11 inch sheet of paper in half along its width. Accordion-pleat each half in 3/8-inch folds. Crease in the middle and spread fanwise. Glue the sides of the two folded papers together, then spread and glue the remaining sides to form a circle. To make the turkey body, fold a 4-inch square of paper diagonally, then open and fold up, about 1 inch, one corner, folding across original diagonal fold. Cut on diagonal fold, from the corner to the corner fold line. Fold the square again and bend outward the triangles formed by the slit. Cut a notch about 1½ inches from the opposite end for the neck. Fold down this end to form the head. Attach the fan tail to the folded-out triangles. Make a V-shaped small notch at the feet to fit on the fold of a heavy-paper or oak tag place card or stand.

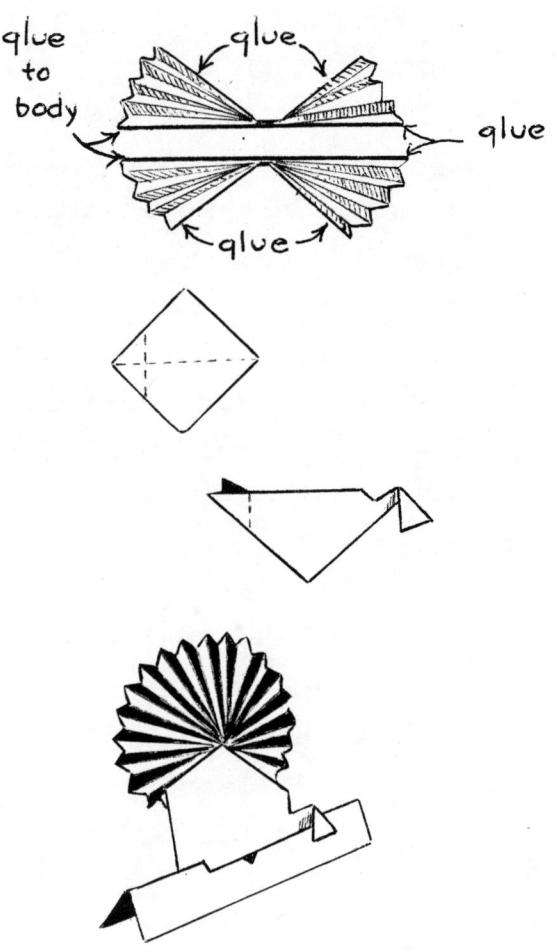

Thanksgiving List

Write "THANKSGIVING" in large, colored letters down the left side of a piece of paper. Use each of these letters to begin a word or phrase of something you are thankful for. Decorate the paper if desired.

WINTER

Cover the Sneeze

    Draw your own head, life-size, on a large piece of paper. Color the hair and eyes to resemble your own. Trace around your hand, color the tracing flesh tone, and cut it out. Staple the hand over a tissue, which covers the nose and mouth, fastening at the wrist only.

Mittens

    Trace around your hands, having the fingers together and the thumb out. Trace partway up the wrist. Decorate the two mittens alike, with stripes, zigzags, dots, or other design. Cut the mittens out and fasten them together at the wrists with yarn.

Chalk Snow Scene

    Make a chalk snow scene with white chalk on blue paper. Use heavy black crayon for accents and outlines, such as shadows under tree branches, fences. Add one small touch of bright red, for a chimney, a scarf, a sled.

Dry-Brush Snow

    Make an outdoor scene with heavy black crayon on blue paper. With very little white paint on a wide brush, carefully draw the brush diagonally across the picture, covering the entire paper. To get the right amount of paint on the brush, dip, then wipe off the excess and test on a piece of extra paper. Brush strokes should show.

Snowflakes

Use black or dark-blue construction paper and lightweight cardboard pieces about 1 inch to 1½ inches wide and approximately 3 inches long. Bend some of the wider strips in two, lengthwise. Dip the narrow end of a cardboard strip into very thick, creamy white paint, getting the paint only on the very edge of the cardboard. Daub onto the paper by pressing the painted edge straight down and form four crossing lines, as shown. Now use a V-shaped bent cardboard strip to paint up and down the spokes, keeping the points of the V toward the center. Add dots by using the corners of the strips, keeping the design symmetrical.

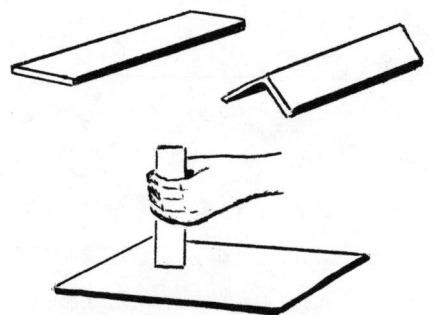

Cutout Six-sided Snowflakes

Fold a square of lightweight paper in half. Bring the bottom corner (next to the fold) three quarters of the way up, to form an angle as shown, then fold the top of the rectangle down and over, lining up the two folds. Cut off the irregular points sticking out. Cut designs and notches along all three sides of the resulting triangle. Cut a deep notch into the side that has no folds. Open.

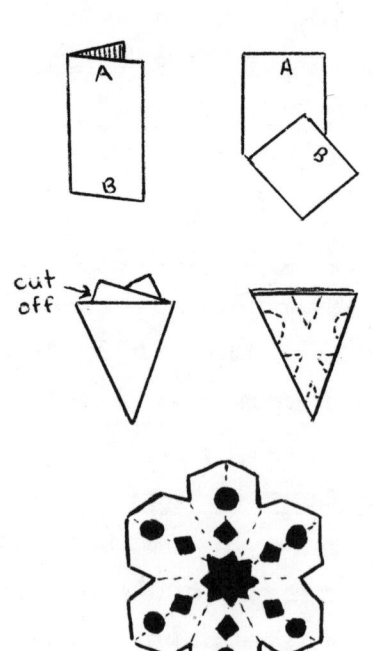

WINTER HOLIDAY IDEAS

Poem to Illustrate

Copy a poem from the board or make up one of your own, about winter or snow. Then make a picture to illustrate it.

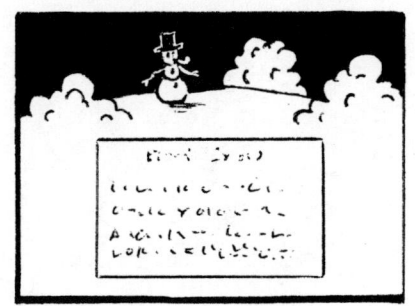

CHRISTMAS

Allover Print

Stick Mystik cloth tape around the edges of any cookie cutter of a Christmas shape. Dip this in paint that has been put into a shallow pan, and print an overlapping, allover design on paper. This could be used to make wrapping paper for gifts.

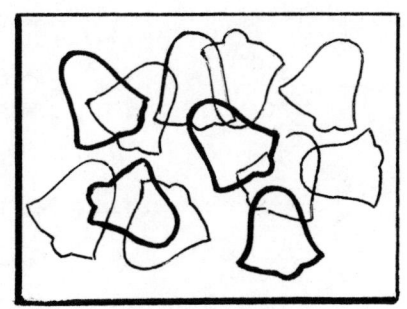

Chain-Link Tree

Make paper link chains in shades of green. Fasten these together and use them to outline a Christmas tree shape on the bulletin board or the wall. Paper ornaments can be added. Use red paper to cut out the tub.

Spiral Tree Mobile

Use a circle of green paper. Cut from the outer edge to the center in a continuous spiral cut. Hang the mobile from the center, so that it will spiral downward.

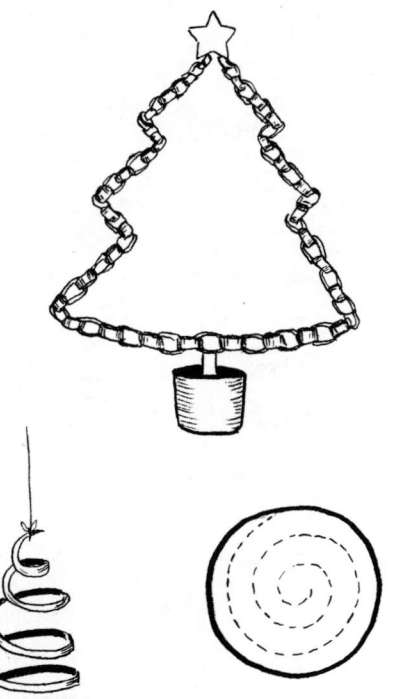

Decorative Coils

Tightly roll narrow strips of colored paper, cut the same length. Glue the ends. When quite a few have been rolled, glue the coils close together in a design, such as a tree shape, bell, star, or abstract design. Glue so that the coiled edges are facing up.

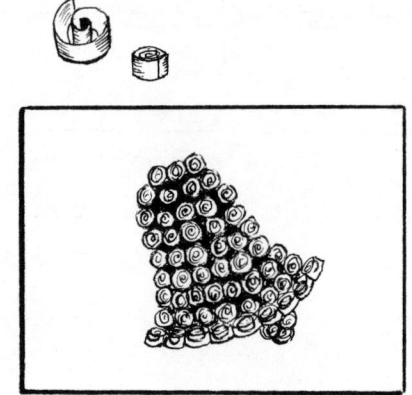

Crumpled Tissue

Cut tissue paper into 2-inch squares. Outline a Christmas design and spread glue in a small part of it. Stick on crumpled tissue paper squares, as close together as possible, choosing colors that will make interesting designs. For a hanging ornament, glue the tissue to both sides of a cutout shape. Add glitter, if desired.

Yarn Tree

Form a paper cone and cover it with wax paper. Dip a 3-foot length of green yarn in liquid starch. Wrap it around the base of the cone several times, then spiral it to the top of the cone. Cut lengths of green yarn about 3 inches longer than the height of the cone. Dip these into the starch and apply from the tip of the cone to the bottom at a slant. Have these strips about an inch apart at the base of the cone. When the yarn is dry, remove the paper cone. Glue pieces of colored tissue between some of the spaces, and add tiny ornaments.

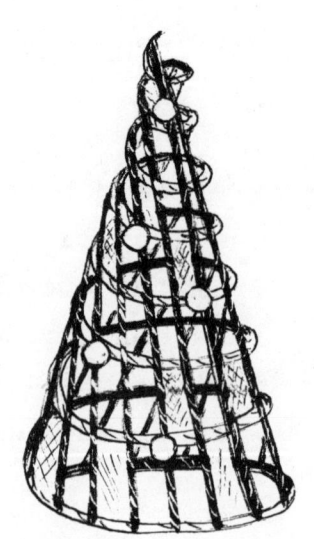

Christmas Ball

   Use nine 4-inch circles of colored paper. Fold each in half and crease it. Open them and stack them together, then staple them together on the crease with three staples. Glue two circle edges together with one drop of glue about one third of the way down from the top. Then, glue the next circle edge with one spot of glue one third of the way up from the bottom. Continue gluing edges together, alternating from the top to the bottom, until the ball is complete.

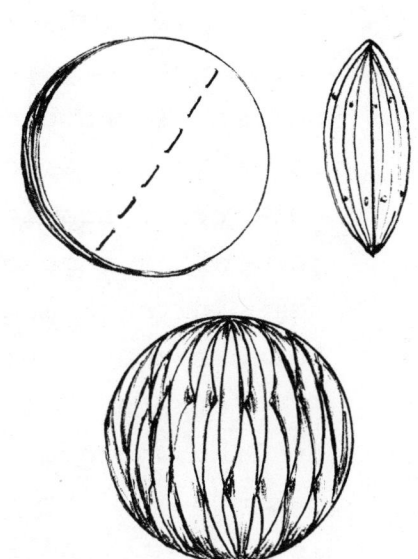

Cellophane Cutouts

   Cut Christmas shapes from a double layer of construction paper. Cut out the center of the shape, leaving about a 1-inch margin of paper. Glue colored cellophane between the two construction-paper shapes. Hang them in front of the windows or fasten them to the glass.

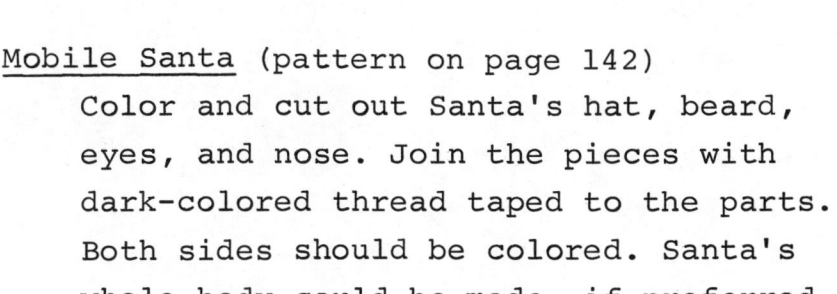

Mobile Santa (pattern on page 142)

   Color and cut out Santa's hat, beard, eyes, and nose. Join the pieces with dark-colored thread taped to the parts. Both sides should be colored. Santa's whole body could be made, if preferred.

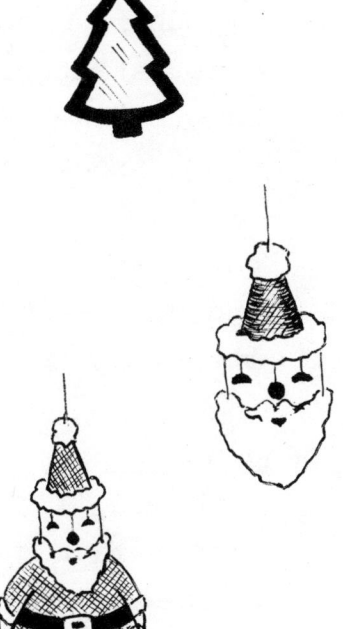

Name Bells

Fold a 12-inch by 18-inch piece of construction paper in half lengthwise. Outline a shape of half a bell, making it as large as possible. Make an identical outline 1 inch inside the first. Placing the folded edge down, write your first name in thick letters, having the letters touch the fold and each other. The letters should also touch the bell outline wherever possible. Carefully cut out all the spaces between the letters and the bell, and from the insides of the letters. Open the paper and hang the bell.

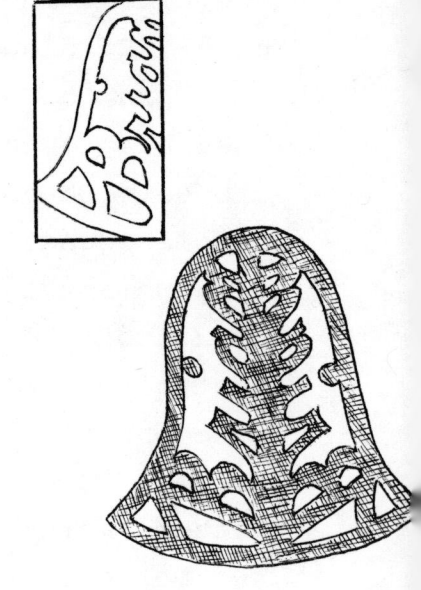

Fringed Tree or Angel

Make a tall paper cone for a base. Cut strips 1 inch by 12 inches and fringe them with 3/4-inch slits close together. Glue these strips around the cone, starting at the bottom and overlapping the rows. Cover the entire cone. For a tree, use green paper and add tiny ornaments. For an angel, use white paper and add cutout head and arms, and glitter on the skirt. Glue wings onto the back.

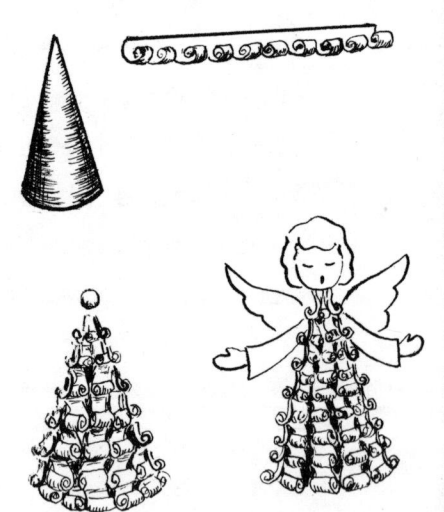

Stand-up Trees

Place one light-green and one darker-green piece of paper together and fold. Draw a half-tree shape and cut it out. Staple along the fold and open the sections outward to form a stand-up tree. It can be fastened to the wall or bulletin board with one side flat against the wall and the other sections folded outward.

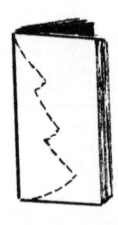

Paper Angels

Fold a 5-inch white paper circle in half. Cut in about 2 inches along the fold from each side toward the center. Cut more slits to outline the bottom of the sleeves and the sides of the head. Fringe above the head and curl for hair. Mark facial features. Roll the bottom of the circle into a cone shape for the skirt and tape or glue.

Candle

Fold a 9-inch by 12-inch piece of paper in half with the 9-inch sides together. Open it. Now bring the top and the bottom edges to the center fold and crease. Cut slits about ½ inch apart from the folded edges toward the center to within about 1 inch from the center. Open the paper and roll it lengthwise. Glue. Add a flame made by cutting a flame shape from two pieces of yellow paper, stapling these together in the center and spreading out the four sides.

Toothpick Ornaments

Glue toothpicks together at the centers only, to form ball or star shapes. Spray paint and glitter them when the glue is dry. Hang them as ornaments.

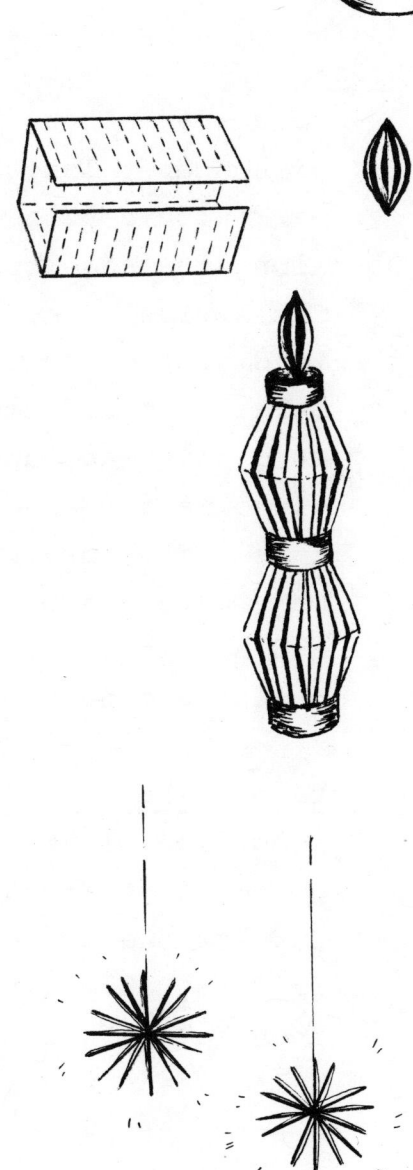

Tissue Mâché Ball

Blow up a balloon to the size of an orange. Using white glue thinned to the consistency of heavy cream, dip bits of colored tissue into it and stick them, overlapping, onto the balloon. Make four to six layers. Smooth the last layer with glue and hang the ball to dry.

Wreath

Fold a 9-inch by 12-inch piece of green paper lengthwise. Lightly mark with pencil a 1-inch margin along the edge opposite the fold. Cut strips ½ inch apart from the fold to the margin line. Fold the margins toward each other and inward, overlap, and glue. Curve the glued margin edge into a circle and fasten it, forming a wreath. Add red berries and a bow. Without the berries and bow, this may be used as a base around a candle or other decoration.

Accordion Pleat Tree

Accordion-pleat a 9-inch by 12-inch piece of green paper lengthwise. Cut off one corner, away from the fold, as shown, then notch about ½ inch below this on the fold. Fasten below the notch and spread to form a star on the top. Spread the bottom to form a tree.

Accordion Angels

Accordion-pleat a piece of white paper, then slit it about one third of the way down the center fold. Refold, then staple it through all thicknesses just below the end of the slit. Fold down the sections on each side of the slit. This forms the angel's arms. Use a paper or ribbon loop for a head. The angel may be hung as a mobile. If made rather small from variegated tissue paper, it makes an attractive tree ornament.

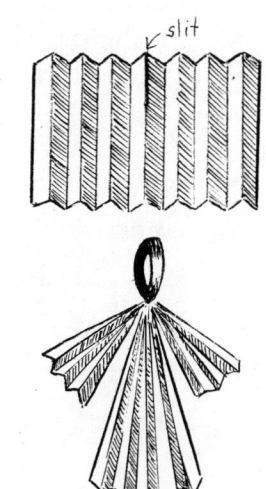

Poinsettias

Pleat a piece of red paper in wide folds, lengthwise, then fold it in half. Trim off one corner, rounding from one edge of the center fold to the opposite corner. Staple in the center on the fold, then open it to form a half circle. Make another in the same manner and fasten them together to make a poinsettia. Paste on yellow circles for centers.

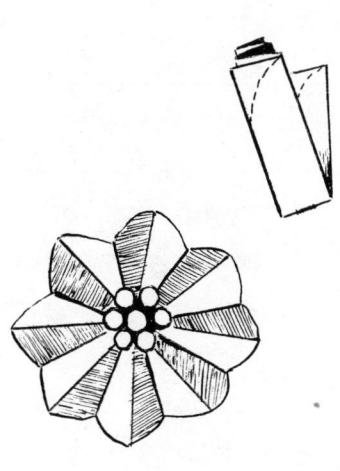

Star

Fold a 9-inch by 12-inch piece of paper in pleats and cut it as shown. Staple the end opposite the point. Make two of these, open and fasten them together to form a star.

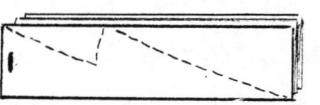

Paper-Strip Mobile

Form circles from strips of colored paper cut the same lengths and glued at the ends. Glue several circles together in an even design. Cut out a candle and glue a yellow flame on it. The flame could be glittered on both sides or cut from gold paper. The candle and flame should be as tall as the paper loops. Make a 1-inch slit in the bottom of the candle and fold these tabs in opposite directions. Glue the tabs to the bottom insides of the loops. Hang it as a mobile.

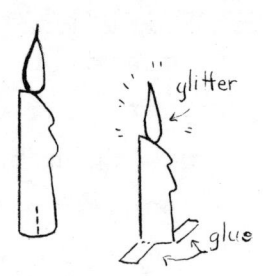

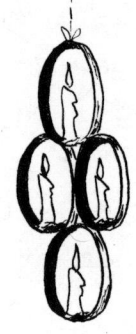

Paper-Strip Stars

Use twelve 1-inch by 12-inch paper strips. Fold each into fourths, bending each fold in the same direction. Overlap and glue the two end quarter sections, forming an even-sided triangle. Glue six of these triangles together, side to side, with points toward the center, as shown. Then glue on the remaining six triangles, making six points. Be sure to hold the sections together until the glue dries, taking plenty of time to finish one section at a time.

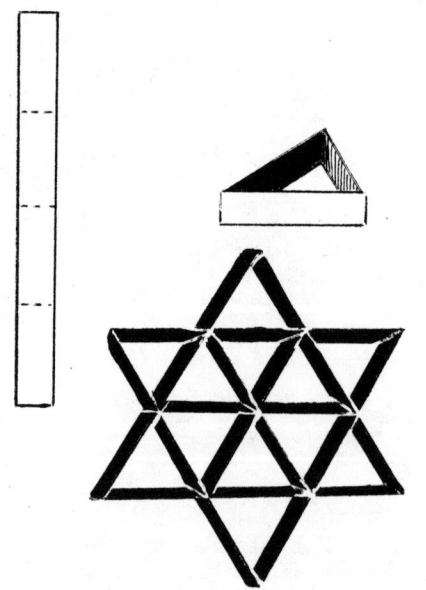

Paper-Strip Tree

Make a tall triangle with a strip of green paper. Completely fill the center with loops made from various-colored paper strips of the same width. Glue these loops to each other and to the sides of the triangle.

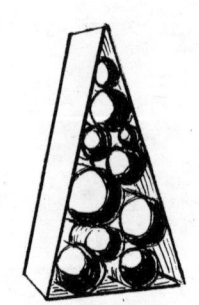

VALENTINE'S DAY

Hanging Hearts

Use six red heart cutouts, about 2 inches long. Print, one word per heart, two of each of the words "I," "love," and "you." Glue a piece of red, pink, or white ribbon between the pairs of hearts. Hang it as a mobile.

Tree of Hearts

Fold a piece of black paper in half. Draw, then cut out, a half-tree shape with many bare branches. Open it and paste it onto a piece of pink paper. Paste red or white heart cutouts on the branches. The hearts should be cut out freehand and of various sizes.

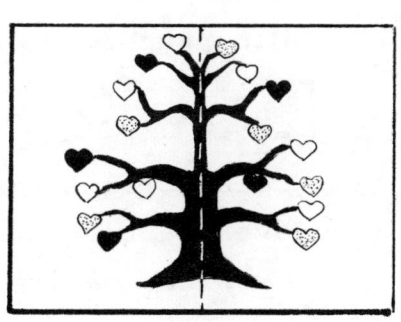

Stuffed Heart Mobile

Paint various sizes of hearts in gay colors and designs, each heart having another matching in size. Staple two hearts together around the bottom edges and stuff with bits of torn paper. Finish, stapling them closed. Using yarn, hang them at different levels and in groups.

Paper Plate Mobile

Use a paper plate with a paper doily pasted in it. Punch holes around the outer edge of the plate. Tie narrow red yarn or ribbon lengths to these holes. Glue red and pink heart shapes to the ends of the ribbon or yarn.

SPRING

Torn-Paper Flowers

Tear a piece of 12-inch by 4-inch green paper to make one of the long sides uneven, resembling grass. Glue this along the edge of a 9-inch by 12-inch piece of blue paper, long, straight edges together. Tear petals, centers, and leaves from brightly colored paper. Color on or cut out stems, then arrange flowers in a pleasing design and glue them onto the blue paper.

Umbrellas

Color bright umbrellas heavily in an all-over pattern on construction paper. Brush over the entire paper with a dry-brush technique, using blue paint and slanting strokes with a wide brush to look like rain. A flat, bristle brush, wiped fairly free of the paint, works best. Test on a piece of scrap paper until brush strokes show.

Iris

Tear in half a 2-inch circle of lavender paper and a 3-inch circle of purple paper. Tear out two long, narrow leaves and cut out a very slightly curved stem. Arrange these to make an iris and glue onto a 4½-inch by 12-inch piece of paper. The lavender circle halves form the upper part of the blossom, the torn edges toward the center, and the purple halves form the lower part of the blossom, the torn edges also toward the center. Add a yellow center.

Pussy Willows

Draw a simple branch shape with brown crayon on brown, gray, or blue paper. Use white chalk to make small, narrow ovals slanting upward and away from the branchlike pussy willow blossoms. Mark a black line along the underside of each oval for a shadow accent. The pussy willows are effective when done on long, narrow paper, then mounted on black.

Kites

Draw a hilltop scene of a boy or a girl with one hand out as though holding a kite string. Color in a blue sky, trees, birds, flowers, or any other spring things. Draw, or paste on, a kite high in the sky. Glue one end of a piece of yarn or string to the kite and the other to the child's hand.

Sit-up Bunny

Fold a piece of white paper and cut out a sitting bunny, with its back on the fold. Cut out two white ears and two smaller pink ear shapes for ear centers. Cut out two pink eyes. Paste centers in ears and paste eyes on the head. Put ends of ears into slits in head and glue them. Add very thin paper whiskers and a fluff of cotton for a tail. Unfold slightly to make the bunny sit up.

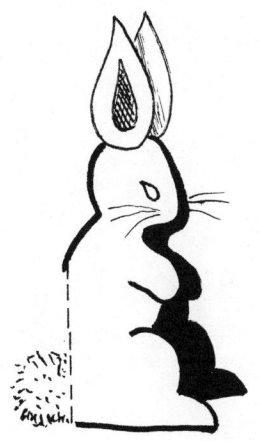

Cutouts

Using colored paper, cut out flower petals, small circles for centers, larger circles to be cut from edge to center in a spiral, little strips to be curled for petals, leaf shapes, stems, and a vase. Make a pleasing flower arrangement and paste it on a colored piece of paper. Instead of having the arrangement in a vase, you could trace around your hand and cut the tracing out, then glue it over the stems of a pasted-on bouquet as though holding it.

Watercolor Petals

Dip all of the brush part of a watercolor brush into a light color of watercolor or tempera paint, using plenty of water. Then dip the point only into a brighter, darker color. Form flower petals by laying the side of the brush on the paper, repeating in a circle, with the wide part of the brush print toward the flower's center. Make a stem, two leaves, and a center for each flower with the tip of the brush.

Eggshell Tulips

Paint the outside and the inside of eggshell halves with pastel colors. Glue these onto a piece of heavy paper, so that the cup of the shell is facing out. Add stems and leaves with crayon, felt-tip pen, or cutouts.

Cloth Flowers

Cut out flower shapes from gaily printed yardage. Paste a solid-colored piece cut in a circle in the center of each flower. Use green cloth for leaves and stems. Cut out a solid-color vase or a burlap flowerpot and glue in an arrangement on a piece of paper.

For March

To illustrate the saying about spring, "In like a lion, out like a lamb," use two paper plates, one for the lion and one for the lamb. For the lion, color or paint a paper plate yellow. Curl yellow paper strips, 1 inch by 3 inches, and glue these close together in two or three overlapping rows around the edge of the plate for the mane. Strips should curl toward the top center of the plate. Paste on black eyes, nose, and mouth, and yellow whiskers. For the lamb, leave the plate white, and paste white paper curls to the top of the plate only. Glue on oval ears, drooping down from the center of the sides. Paste on black eyes, nose, and mouth. The lamb would have no whiskers.

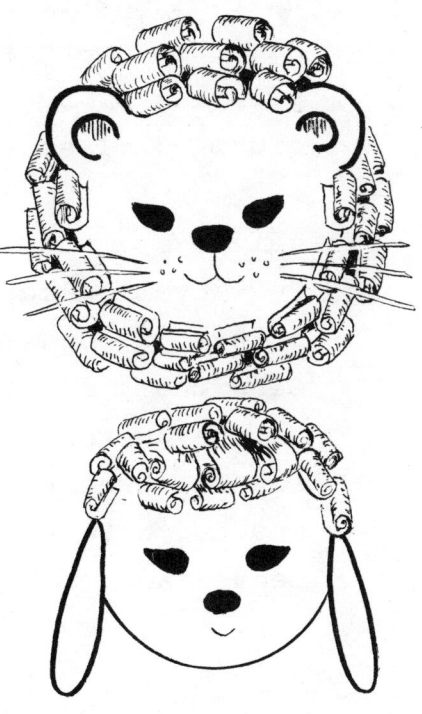

Hyacinth

Use little wads of tissue or crepe paper in shades of lavenders and purples and pinks. Glue these very close together in a long oval shape to resemble hyacinth blossoms. Add a stem and long, narrow leaves.

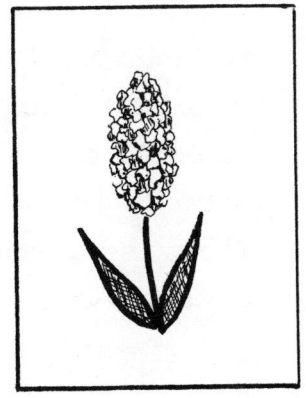

Straw Blow

Cut a piece of 9-inch by 12-inch pale-colored construction paper in half, lengthwise. Drop one drop of black or brown paint about an inch from the bottom. With a soda straw held very close to the paint and at an angle, blow the drop of paint so that it travels up the length of the paper and branches out to look somewhat like a tree or a branch. Make blossoms on these branches by sponge painting or by gluing on bits of crumpled tissue paper.

Daffodils

Cut a yellow cupcake paper in half and bring cut edges of each half together. Glue them, forming the cuplike center of the daffodil. Paste the center, or several centers, to a piece of paper and add cutout yellow petals, green leaves and stems.

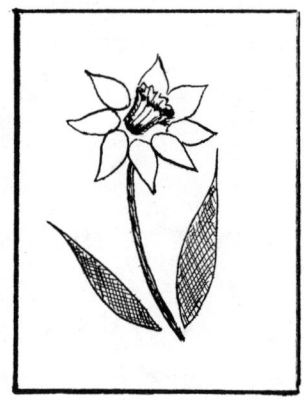

Umbrella

Cut wedge shapes from pastel-colored pieces of paper. Roll these into rather narrow cones and glue to hold. Arrange these cones, points together, in an umbrella shape. Add a cutout handle. Glue 1-inch lengths of plastic drinking straws onto the background, at a slant, to represent rain. This is effective done in a large scale on a bulletin board.

Egg Mobile

Paint or color several paper plates in pastel colors, and punch five holes around the rims. Colorfully decorate egg shapes, about 3 or 4 inches in length. Staple or glue partway around the edges of two eggs, then stuff with bits of crumpled paper. Glue or staple the rest of the edges. Suspend the eggs from the paper plates with yarn or ribbon.

Egg Tree

Blow a drop of black ink or paint by holding a drinking straw close to the drop at a slant. Use any color of pastel shade for the paper. Blow the paint into branch or tree shapes. When the paper is dry, paste on colored and decorated eggs. This can be accented nicely by gluing a strip of black paper to the top and the bottom of the picture or by mounting it on black paper.

Crayon Resist

Draw and color Easter eggs very heavily with wax crayons. Dip the entire paper into a tray of diluted paint of a dark color. Let the paint run off. Or spoon the paint onto the paper, then tip the paper back and forth to achieve a runny effect.

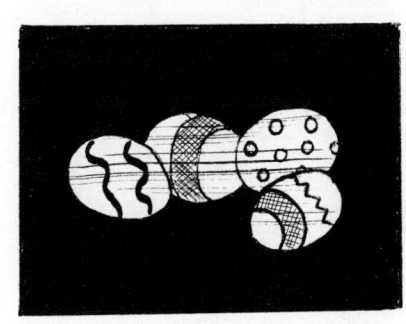

Transparent Eggs

Cut two large egg shapes from wax paper. Using very small dabs of glue, fasten overlapping bits of pastel-colored tissue to one egg shape. Cover with the other egg shape, and press with an iron. Crayon scrapings may be used also.

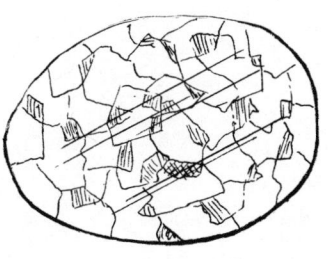

Outlines for Patterns or Duplicating Masters

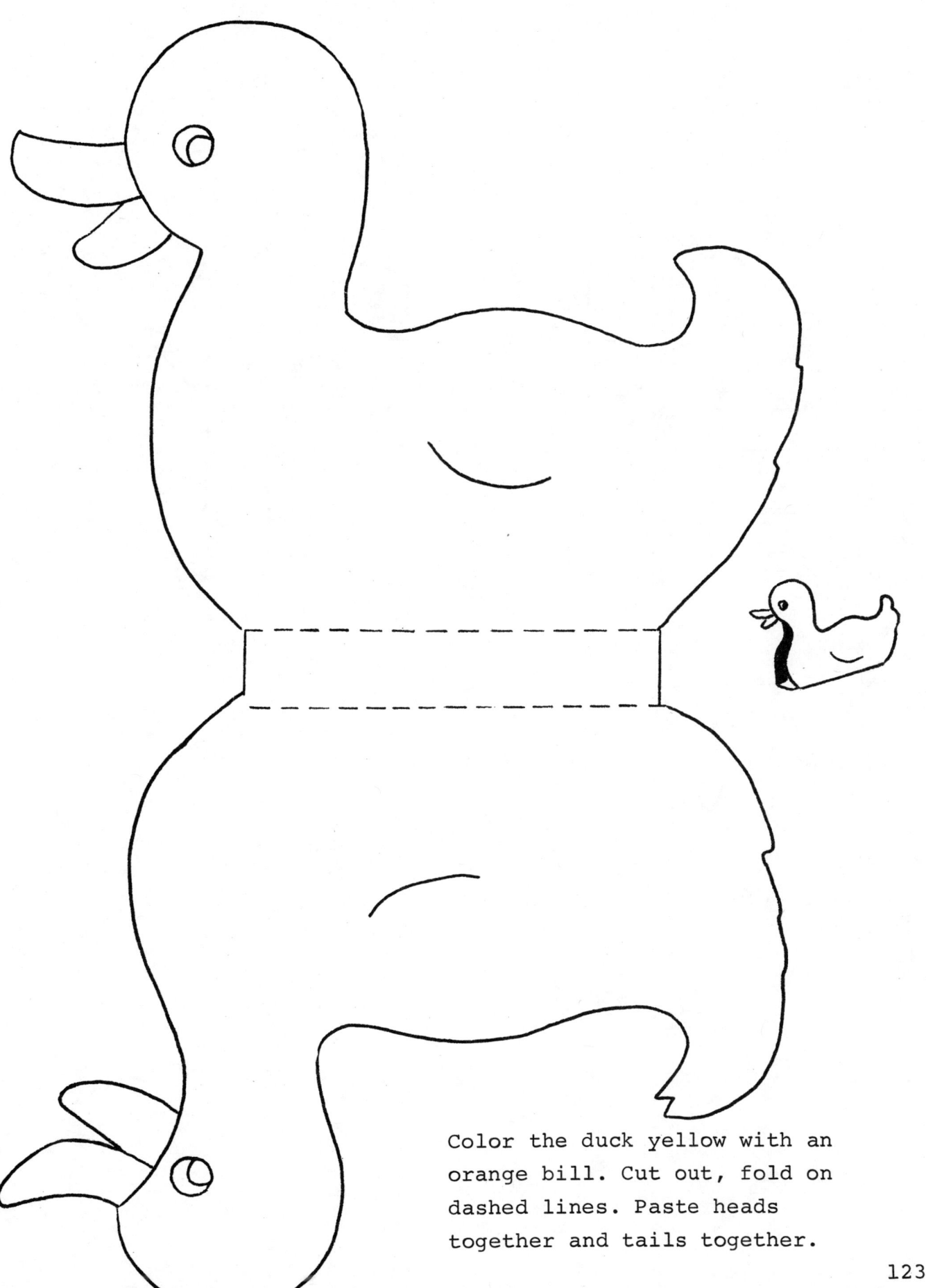

Color the duck yellow with an orange bill. Cut out, fold on dashed lines. Paste heads together and tails together.

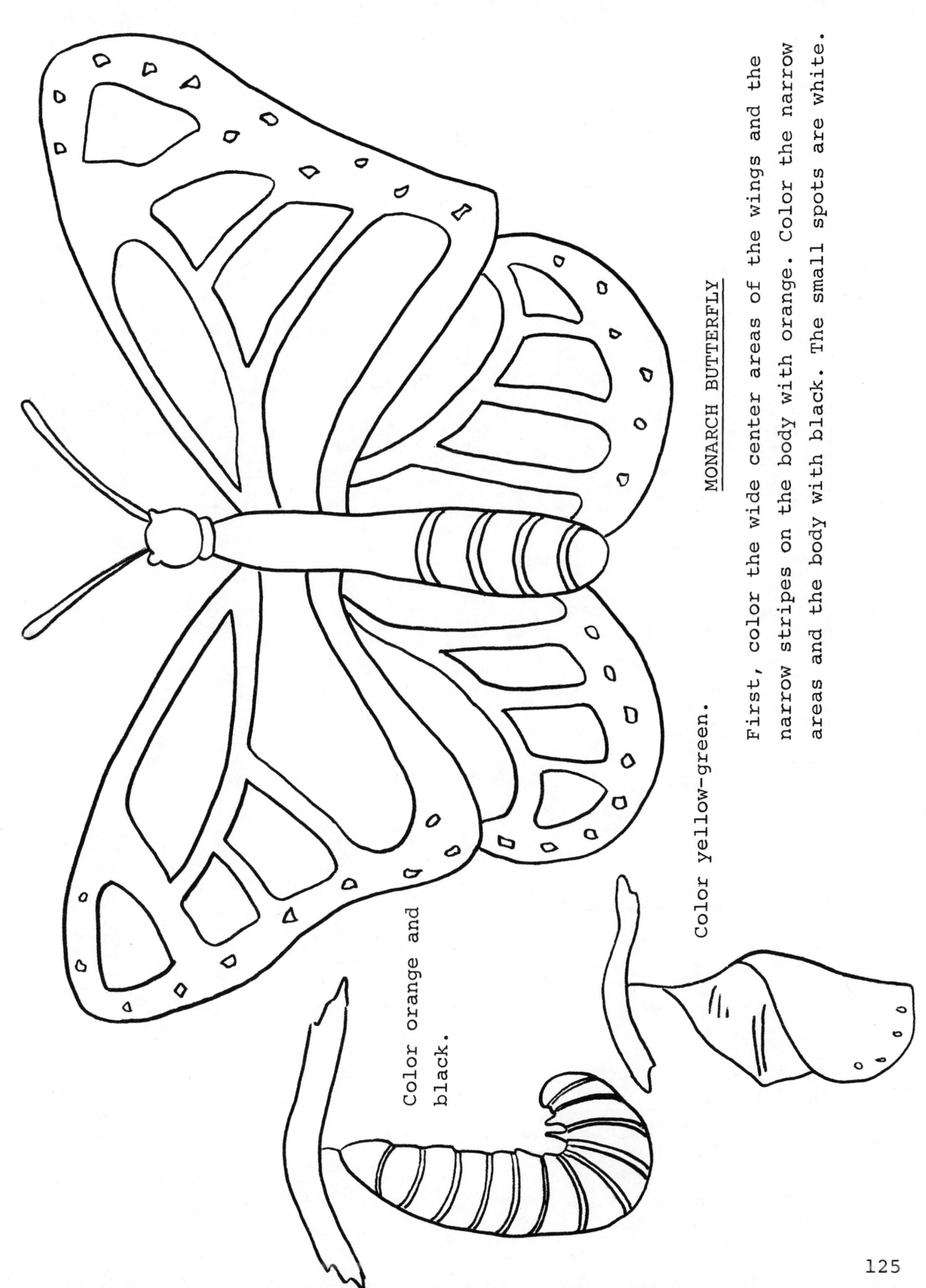

MONARCH BUTTERFLY

First, color the wide center areas of the wings and the narrow stripes on the body with orange. Color the narrow areas and the body with black. The small spots are white.

Color yellow-green.

Color orange and black.

Across
1. You read from _____.
3. To find the sum, you _____.
5. It rings.
6. In art you _____.
7. You sit at a _____.
10. Use ____ on the blackboard.
11. Sit on a _____.
12. Write on ____.
14. The date is on the _____.

Down
1. Eat _____ before coming to school.
2. Have a _____ for lunch.
4. Sleep on a _____.
8. If it's not right, _____ it.
9. Measure with a _____.
12. Write with a _____.
13. You hear with your _____.

Use with pages 89 and 92.

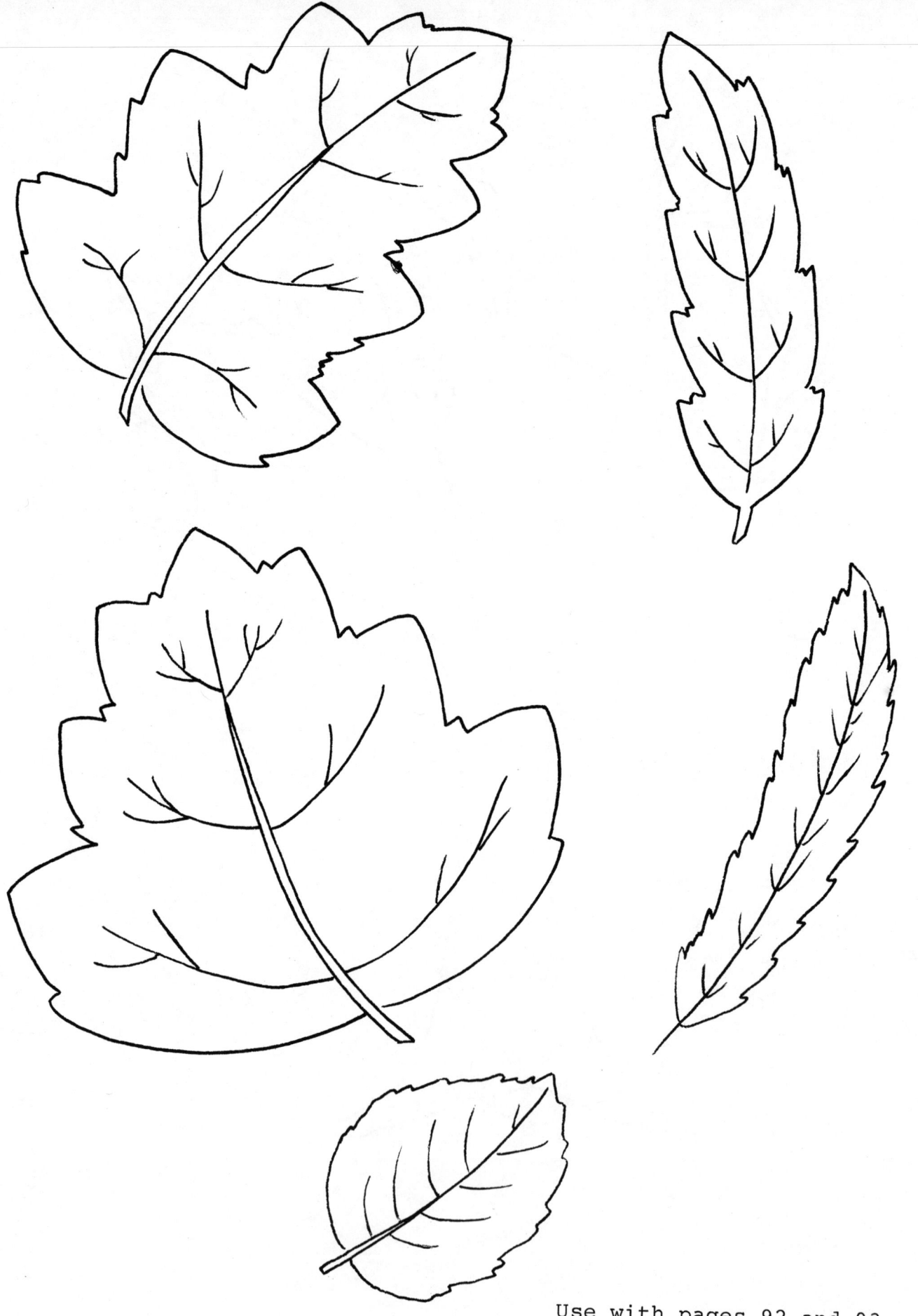

Use with pages 92 and 93.

Use with page 93.

Use with page 93.

Use with page 93.

Use with page 95.

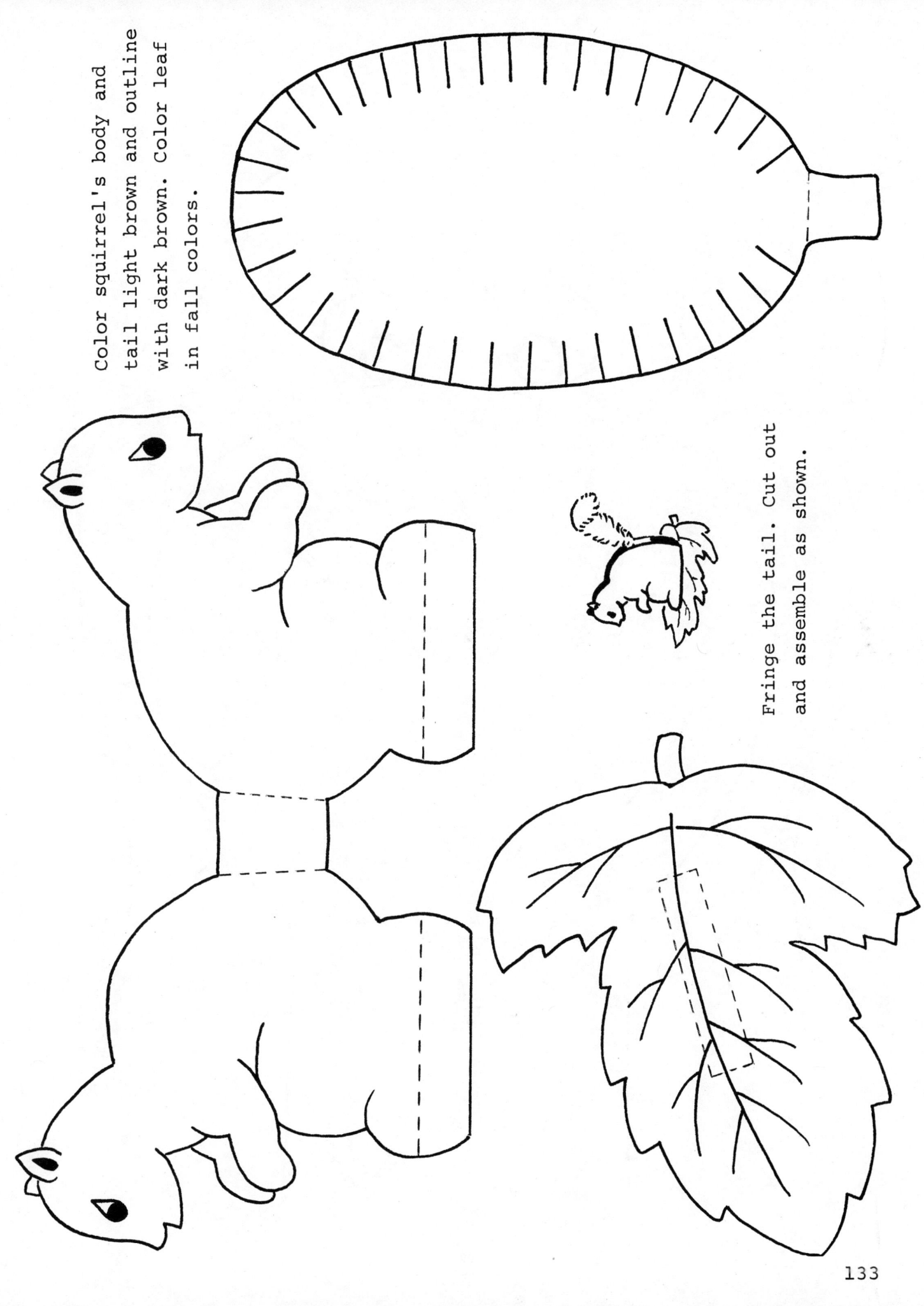

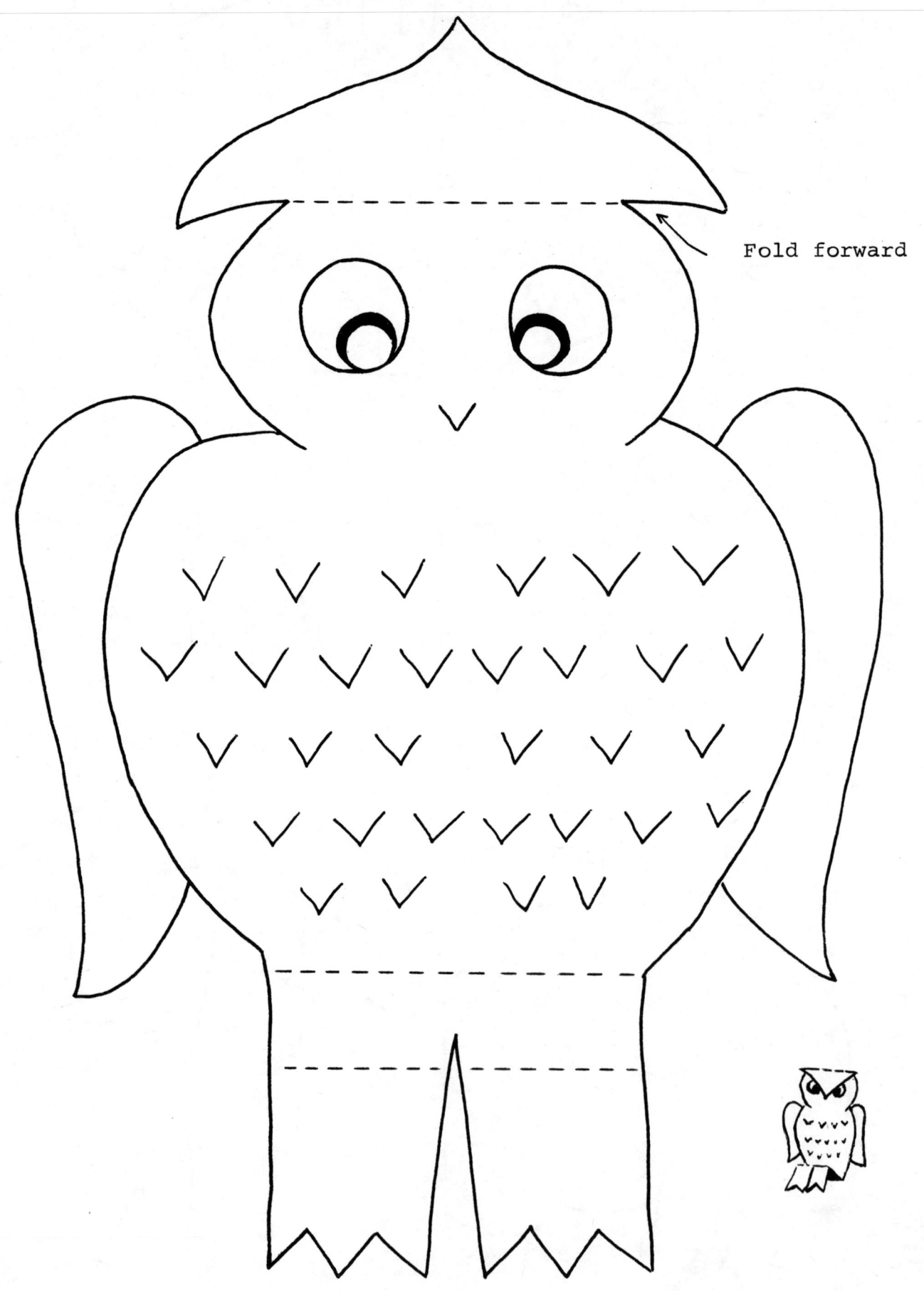

Fold forward

Use with page 103.

Cut out these shapes from a double layer of dark-colored construction paper. Paste a piece of bright-colored tissue or cellophane between the two construction paper outlines. Hang the designs in front of windows or lights, or fasten them to the glass.

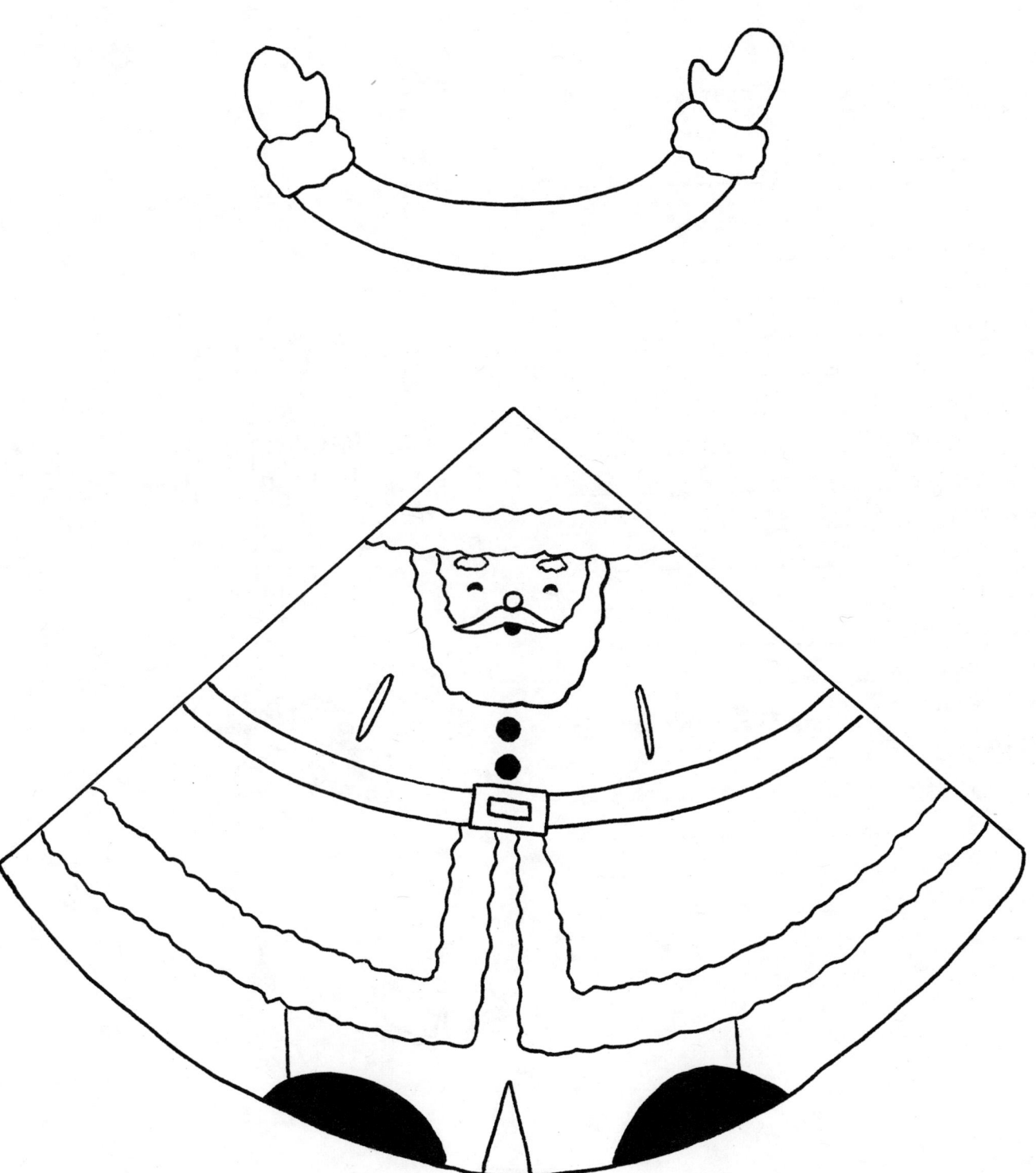

Copy this on red construction paper. Color beard, brows, and trim on hat and coat with white chalk, or glue on cotton. Roll into cone and fasten. Slip arms through slits from the back.

Unscramble these Christmas words:

1. slebl _____
2. stilgh _____
3. eter _____
4. slacor _____
5. wons _____
6. hhrucc _____
7. strepnes _____
8. kiscotgn _____
9. stana _____
10. yoj _____
11. rats _____
12. gramen _____
13. saglen _____
14. nobbris _____
15. daync _____
16. redenier _____
17. deshrepsh _____
18. lone _____
19. yots _____
20. glishe _____

Cut along outer edges of wings, body, and book. Cut on the lines between arms and skirt. Roll the skirt into a cone and fasten it. Bring arms forward and paste to songbook. Slip wings onto the back of the skirt.

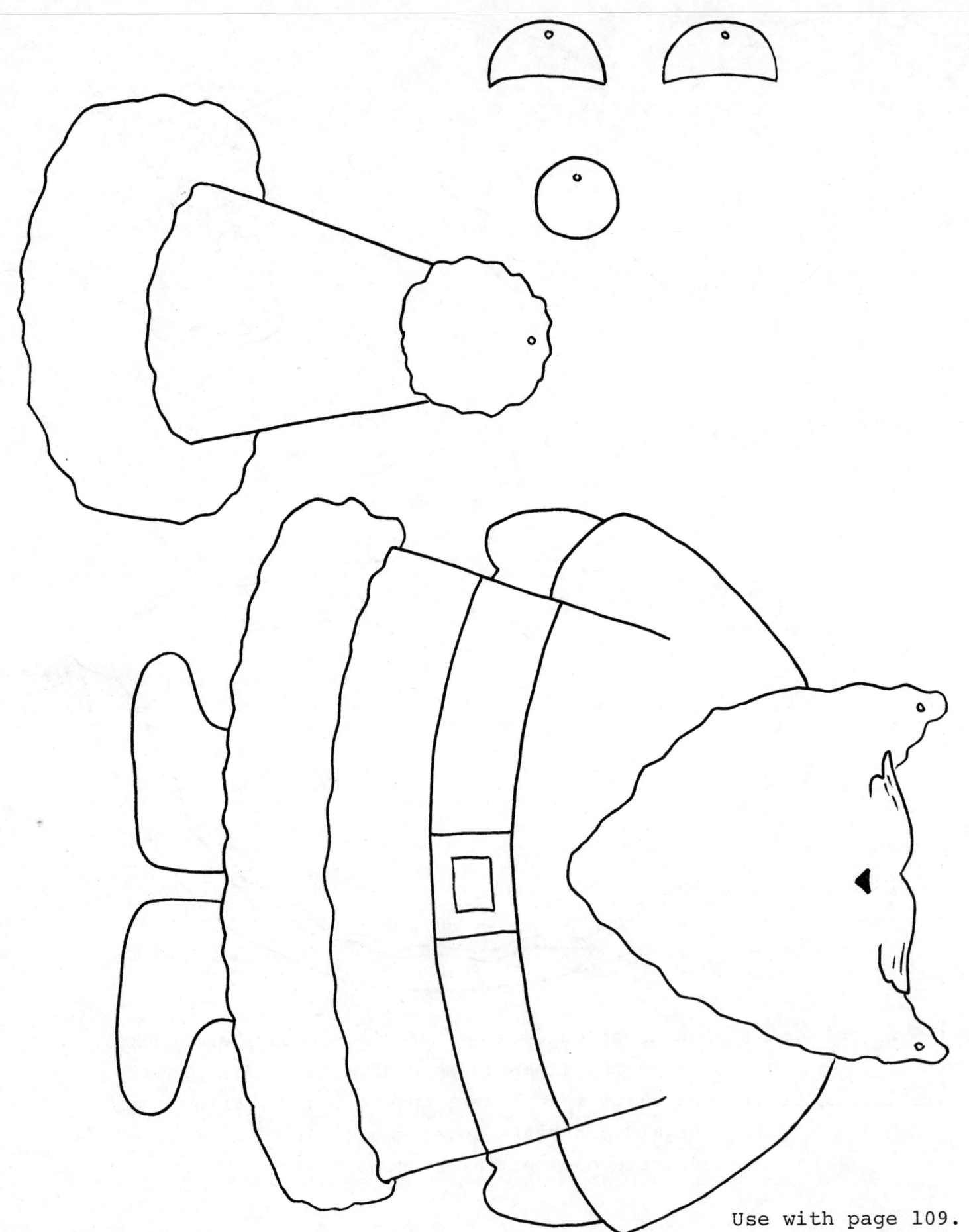

Use with page 109.

142

Fold on dashed lines and paste to form body.
Cut all slits and curl. Fasten wings to body.
Hang by center top.

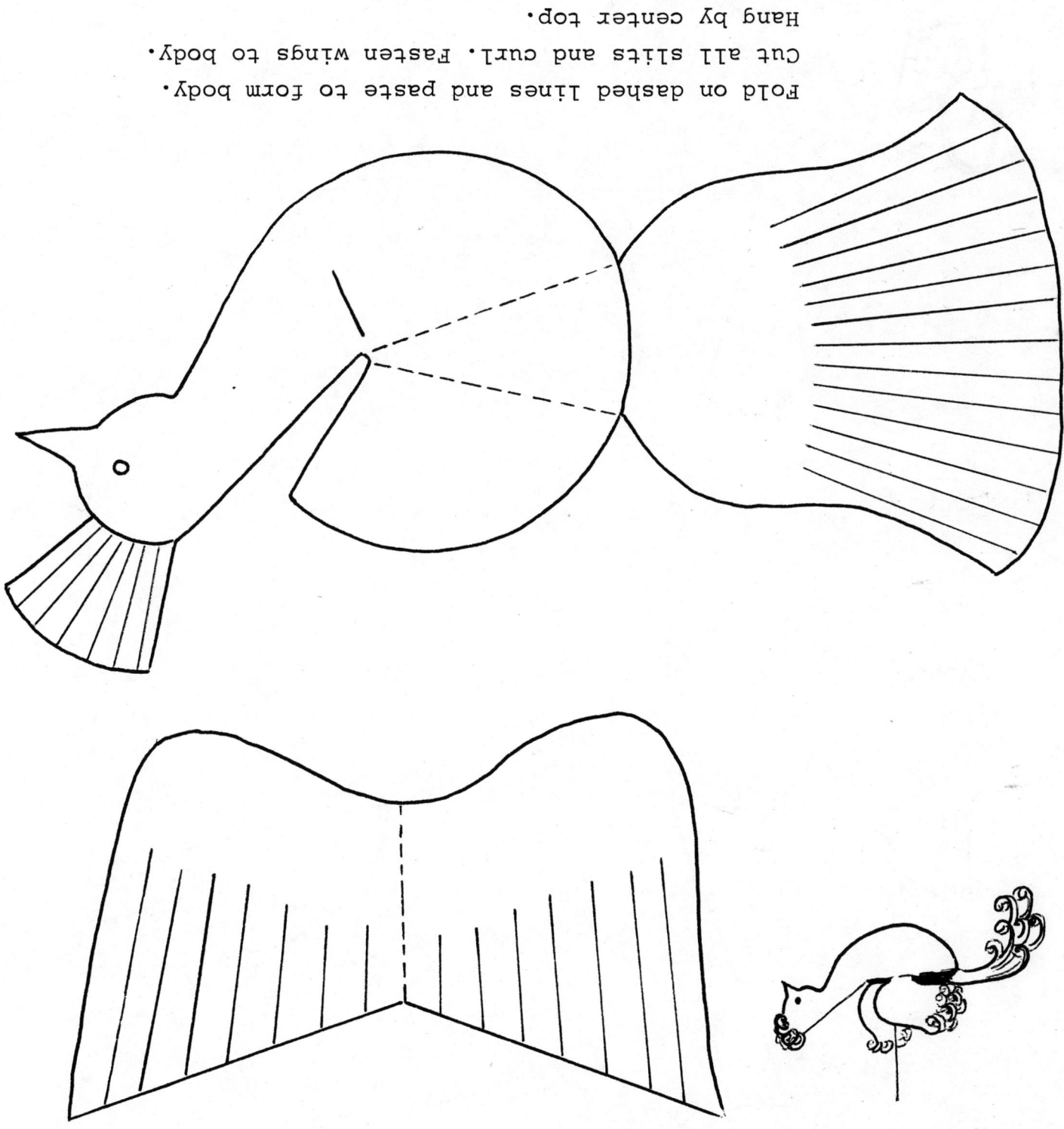

143

Print on a light shade of paper. Color or paste on decorations. Fasten by putting tabs in slits. Glue on or staple on a handle.

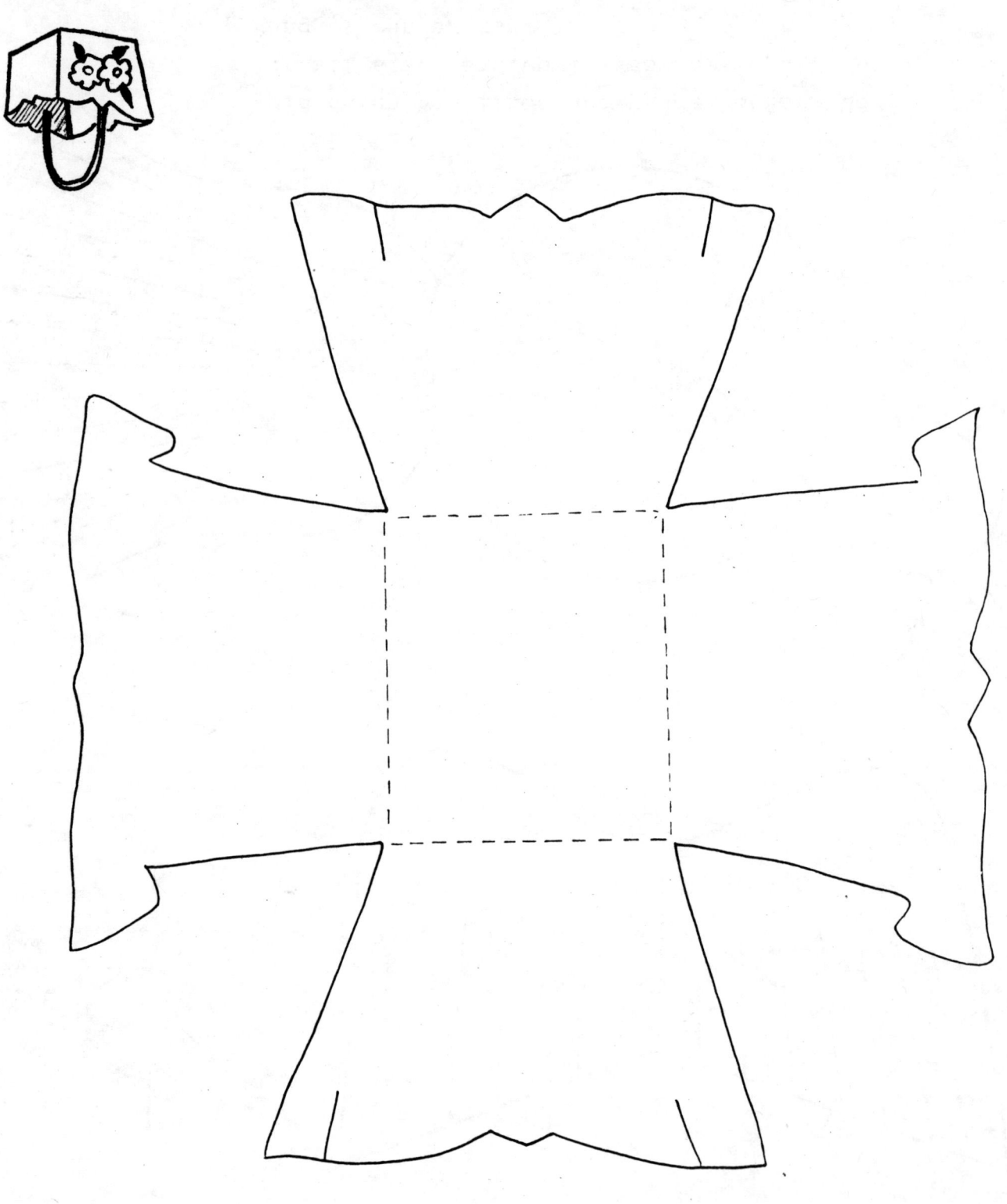

MAY BASKET

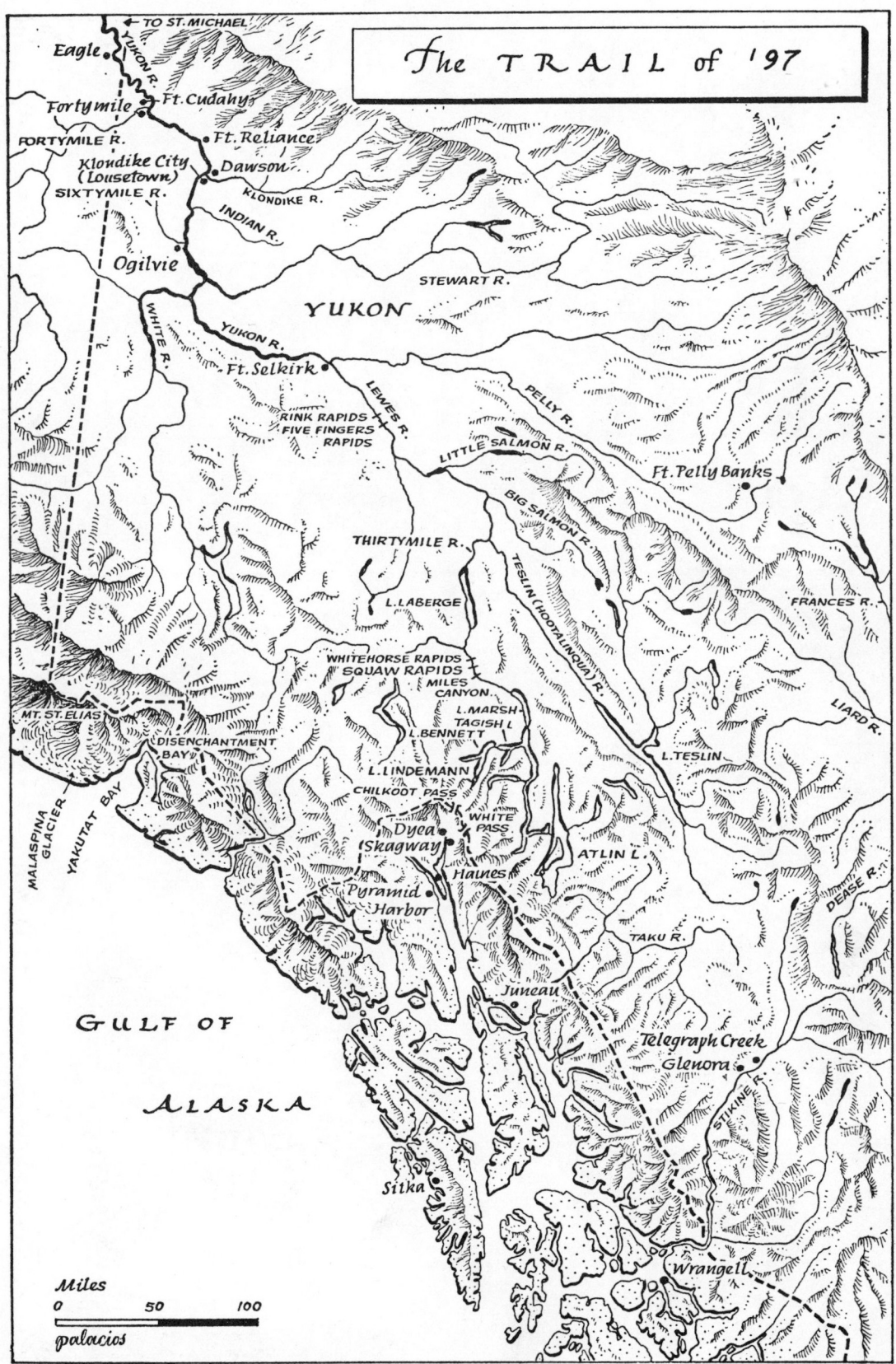